SOMETHING
CHANGED

STUMBLING THROUGH DIVORCE,
DATING & DEPRESSION

Published in paperback in 2017 by Sixth Element Publishing
on behalf of Matthew Williams

Sixth Element Publishing
Arthur Robinson House
13-14 The Green
Billingham TS23 1EU
Tel: 01642 360253
www.6epublishing.net

ISBN 978-1-912218-14-1

British Library Cataloguing in Publication Data. A catalogue record for this book is
available from the British Library.

Printed in Great Britain.

1 2 3 4 5 6 7 8 9 0

SOMETHING CHANGED

STUMBLING THROUGH DIVORCE, DATING & DEPRESSION

MATTHEW WILLIAMS

To my beautiful children, Gracie & Gabe,
some things will never change.

'You can't connect the dots looking forward; you can only connect them looking backwards. So you have to trust that the dots will somehow connect in your future. You have to trust in something — your gut, destiny, life, karma, whatever.'

Steve Jobs

CONTENTS

Part 3
Dating, Bloody Hell:
Dispatches from The Rocky Road to Romance

Part 4
Daddy: Thoughts from a Single Dad

Part 5
Today: Standing at a Crossroads

Epilogue

ACKNOWLEDGEMENTS

There are many people without whom this book would not have been possible and I would like to offer some specific thanks:

To my family – Mam, Dad, Dan and Oliver – for everything.

To Dan – the true talent of the family – special thanks are owed for the wonderful artwork. You see me.

To Woody, for believing in me when I was at my lowest and didn't believe in myself. You told me I could write a book, who would have guessed you would be right?

To Nichola, for helping me to know myself better than I ever have before and for everything you have done to help me along the path to discovering my true self.

To Di, for being the final catalyst for the publication of my first book.

To Rachael, for being a good friend and my blog's most loyal supporter.

To 'Our Rach' for your advice and encouragement in the early days of my blog. Our Rach is still my favourite blog! (www.ourrachblogs.com)

To everybody that has supported me by reading my blog and encouraging me in my writing, especially in the difficult early days. You are too numerous to mention but you know who you are. Thank you.

PREFACE:
SOMETHING CHANGED

'Thousands of pounds for a piece of paper...'

Cynics often voice this opinion when asked to consider the value of marriage. In a bitter irony you could say exactly the same thing about divorce, only the signing of the papers takes place without ceremony and the cost is counted in far more than pounds and pence.

I always wanted to get married. I've always had a strong sense of the importance of family and for me marriage was an important step in becoming a family. I don't presume to judge how anybody else chooses to live, but it's important to me. And everything about my wedding was wonderful – the stag do (a world title fight, a natural for a boxing nut), the honeymoon (Las Vegas – and an early act of self-sacrifice in forgoing the opportunity to be part of the crowd for the fight scenes for 'Rocky Balboa' which were being filmed on day one of the honeymoon), and, above all, the wedding day itself.

Sound advice from friends helped to create the perfect day: the day goes quickly, make sure you take it all in; when circulating to talk to all of your guests make sure you don't spend too much of the day away from each other, and select the menu yourself instead of offering options – it will save you having to chase people up for their choices (soup and chicken, you can't go wrong). Of course, there were 'moments' in the planning stages (the usual, you know, arguments with family about guests), but all of that was forgotten about on the big day.

Sunday 4th December 2005

It was, well, it was perfect. Everything I could have hoped for and more. And, as a music lover the soundtrack had to be perfect, and so it was. Our first dance, Pulp's 'Something Changed'. A song from one of my favourite albums, released a week before we met and a soundtrack to those early days; a song quoted in her first Christmas card to me. A song that became tied to a dance that felt every bit an act of love timetabled by someone up above.

Fast forward, Tuesday 5th August 2014

The day began as a significant day for me – a year to the day that I had returned to work after my second bout of severe depression, the first having struck me down during our first year of marriage. I had no way of knowing that my life was about to dramatically change course and I was completely unprepared for the new significance that this date was about to assume. A date that would mark the beginning of a very different life. The date that 'Till death do us part' became a hollow echo from the past, empty of the promise that it once held. The date that my marriage died.

The truth is that my marriage must have been dying long before that. I didn't see it, or maybe I just didn't want to see it. There had been warnings but somehow I really hadn't faced up to them. In some ways I couldn't face up to them. I was blinded to my wife's unhappiness, blinded by my own belief in what marriage is: by my belief that my marriage would be for life, by the rock solid conviction that now we had children nothing would tear us asunder. I was wrong. Only realising that fact once it was too late is one of the hardest things I have ever had to face. Yes, there are regrets, but at a distance removed from that time, it is easy to look back at what could have, perhaps what should have been. Whatever led us to that fork in the road – at that time and for reasons I will probably never fully understand – it determined that our futures lay apart. Our sacred lifelong bond was broken. And it couldn't (or perhaps wouldn't?) be repaired.

I don't know the official date that my marriage ended, the date that the decree absolute was passed. It doesn't matter, my marriage died the day that my wife told me that she no longer loved me. At least that's the day it died for me. But my belief in marriage never died; marriage was never a piece of paper to me and I still remember taking my vows, how deeply and sincerely I meant them. Being married – after ten years together – meant something. It felt different. It felt special. In marriage I believe that love isn't just a feeling – indeed, at times it may not be a feeling at all – it is a daily decision to face life, to navigate its peaks and valleys, together. It is a decision that we had taken for nearly nine years.

Where would I be now if we hadn't met on that day so many years ago? For most of us, any contemplation of this question on our wedding day leads us only to that day, the happiest day of our lives. Wherever we would be it wouldn't be here, and here is the only place we want to be. Upon divorce the question inevitably leads us to an altogether different form of contemplation – at what point in our journey could we have taken a different turn, a turn that would have avoided the signpost to divorce? Or perhaps a turn that would have steered us away from this sudden adversary disguised as the person we married? But that path leads us nowhere for, once in our lives, that person was everything we wanted. And while acutely and painfully aware of what we have lost, we must not lose sight of what was gained; not only in joining together, but also in facing the challenges of breaking apart.

This is a story of facing those challenges, of starting over again and finding new meaning and new purpose in life. It is a story of coming to terms with divorce and becoming a single father. Of facing the spectre of mental illness, and of riding the rollercoaster of modern dating. It is a story of looking inside and facing the demons that live there.

This is my story.

PART 1

WHEN THE LOVE STOPS: DEALING WITH DIVORCE

HERE GOES...

It's funny how life can be. In December 2015 I felt a compulsion to write. I was going through a difficult time after an arduous few years that included a severe depression and a divorce. That week it would have been my tenth anniversary. One of the family cats, part of the family that I lost, had just died. My ex-wife's new partner was moving in with her and my children. The woman I'd had a brief relationship with after my marriage ended had started dating somebody new. And my first Christmas alone was looming.

I'd never written expressively before but on this particular evening, alone in a Travelodge in Tamworth, I sat down and I typed. I really didn't know what I would say, just that I had to write to make some sort of sense of the thoughts, feelings and emotions that swirled inside of me. Writing was to be my catharsis, my way of avoiding the slide into the blackness that had engulfed me previously. I was going to make it into a blog (even though I had no idea of how to create a blog). So I began:

Well, hello, I guess. At this point I expect I am talking to a vast empty space but hey-ho we've all got to start somewhere. So, why blog, and why now?

I've toyed with the idea of blogging for over a year now, since I started feeling almost human again after my whole world was tipped upside down when my then wife told me that our marriage was over. In the year since my break-up, two things have loomed

7

large in my life – divorce and dating. If I'm honest another big, dark D lurks in the background – depression; thankfully two break-ups in the last eighteen months haven't led to a third breakdown.

Why blog now? Well, post-divorce life is a rollercoaster of emotions, of good experiences and bad, of lessons learned and loves lost. Glowing optimism gives way to deep loneliness only for rays of hope to shine through again. Often within days. This seems to be my life's playlist and it's playing on repeat. For me, equally cursed and blessed with a brain that over-thinks and a lot of time for it to do its best and its worst, this blog offers an opportunity to make sense of the maelstrom of thoughts, feelings and emotions that divorce and dating bring. It also offers me the opportunity to learn, to use my experiences to become a better person, a better parent and hopefully, in time, a better partner. To the right partner.

Is this something that many men do? I expect not, apparently expressing our deepest hopes and fears, sharing our highs and lows and opening ourselves emotionally is not the done thing for us men. Well, I say fuck that. We're human, we all feel these things to a greater or lesser degree and whether tens of people or thousands of people read this, I hope that somehow, something that I say will connect with somebody, will act as a light in sad times, and provide some laughs along the way.

I'm a lover of a good quote; with the advent of social media we see inspirational quotes every day – well, if that's your thing, one person's inspiration is another's clichéd bollocks I guess – and I will end my first ever blog with one of my favourites (and my next tattoo), from the late, great US comedian Bill Hicks:

'Don't worry, don't be afraid, ever, because this is just a ride.'

It's one thing feeling touched by inspiration when we are happily going about our days, it's another thing entirely to hold on to your belief in such words when life hits you where it hurts. But you know what? If there's one thing that life has taught me in my forty one years, it's that things have a way of working out. And in the rear-view mirror of our lives our blackest days can reveal themselves to be signposts to a better future to be enjoyed by a wiser version of ourselves.

Why now? I missed the real reason. This week has been the shits for me. I am hurting like I haven't hurt for a long time. But I can't allow myself to wallow in it; it will pass, I will learn, and as sure as day follows night, life will continue with all of the ups and downs that create the rich tapestry of our own personal stories.

Here's mine.

After downloading a blogging app, I released my thoughts into the world and I wondered… wondered whether the whole thing was a bit, well, trite and self-pitying, given the huge suffering that we see in the world and in the lives of others. Yes, I had doubts about what I was doing, after all it's not every day that you decide to place your thoughts and feelings out there for all to see. I've always said that I don't care what others think of me and to an extent that is true – when all is said and done I've largely followed my own path in life. But can I really say that I'm not bothered by what anybody else thinks? Of course not. We are social animals and a large part of how we define ourselves is by the relationships that we have and the way that we are perceived by others. And I'd rather be perceived positively thank you very much.

We can't control how others will judge us nor allow ourselves to become preoccupied with what others think to the extent that we begin to turn in on ourselves, giving free rein to the negative voice that we all have. As I've learned to my own cost, it will be more than happy to do its worst given the opportunity. I was, and at times remain, conscious that people will judge me based on the way I express my thoughts and feelings to the world. I caught myself wondering whether one day in the future (or on many days…) I would read my words back to myself and cringe, wondering what the fuck I was thinking. Who knows, but at that time I knew that writing was good for me and was helping me a great deal. We have to follow our own instincts and for some reason mine told me that I had to write. Not that I should, or that I might want to, but that I had to.

Once the floodgates of my brain were opened and the words began to flow, they weren't about to stop. It seemed I had a lot of shit just waiting to be let out.

WHEN THE LOVE STOPS: PART 1

When the love stops
Hopes lost
Gone is our forever
Promises made
That we'd stay
Together whatever the weather

Till death do us part
Blown apart
Promises in tatters
Solemn vows
A love that's bound
For eternity, now shattered

Devastation hits
A tonne of bricks
Desperation writ upon me
Where to turn
How to learn
To live without her beside me

A dismantled life
Cut like a knife
The ties that bind, severed
Future days
An unfamiliar shape
Drifting, alone, untethered

I WUZ ROBBED!

Two of the more surreal incidents in my life involve being robbed. The first of these was in London around sixteen years or so ago (when I bought my first drink. Boom boom). Well, it was about as blatant as the everyday robbery that is London prices anyway. I was mugged by some apparent drug addict in broad daylight on one of London's busiest streets in the middle of the day. The guy loudly demanded money that I told him I didn't have, despite having a £5 and £10 note in my pocket, so he proceeded to march me to a cash machine to draw some out for him. He did kindly offer me a spliff for my trouble but I politely declined. Germs and that.

I remember feeling very calm throughout and considering my options. The best seemed to be smacking him and running away but I was on my way for a weekend back home in the North East and was carrying a heavy bag that I couldn't lug about in a chase. As he was clearly not the most stable of individuals there was also an obvious risk involved. So, I found myself following him up the street looking for a cash machine watching the multitudes of people passing by while thinking to myself how bizarre the whole situation was. In the end I couldn't be arsed with it and told him I had a train to catch so I'd give him a note from my pocket. Reaching blindly into it I pulled out the… £10. Of course, cheers. Still, I got my train and presumably he got as high as a kite. All's well that ends well.

The second incident was even more surreal. I'd had a long

day working in London and returned to Darlington train station around 9.30pm. As I returned to my car, something looked off and I noticed that all of my paperwork was scattered on the backseat. I went to put my bag in the boot before checking things out, when I noticed movement in the car. Yup, some filthy scummer was in my car rifling through my things. Fair to say it wasn't quite as pleasant a surprise as the time an admiring passer-by had left a note with her phone number on my windscreen.

I used the button on my keys to make sure he was locked in and called the police, at which point I heard a noise and noticed my scruffy new acquaintance sliding his drug-addled semi-corpse through the smashed driver's window. My options appeared before me in a PlayStation RPG-esque slow motion time capsule.

'Get out of my FUCKING car!!!' I growled, with as much menace as I could muster.

'Is this yours?' (Errrrr, well it ain't yours, is it, shithead?)

'Yeah, now put my things down and FUCK OFF!' (Scruffer shuffles forward, puts hand in pocket).

'I'm going to stab you.'

You know what? He might have had a satnav and some sunglasses of mine but I had two beautiful children at home. He didn't have much to lose judging by the clip of him. I wasn't going to risk dying in a pool of blood in a shitty car park in Darlington in the pissing rain soundtracked by the groans of nearby cattle. So I ran, enough so he wouldn't catch me but all the while keeping him in my sights to get a good description. He was caught – an addict that had plenty of previous and was well-known to police – and I got my stuff back. He got a community order and I got £100 compensation deposited sporadically in my bank account a few pennies at a time until I'm about eighty seven. That'll teach him. (It didn't actually, he was in front of the magistrate again the following year and they sent me a letter asking me if I would let him off paying what he owed me. Errrr, good thinking, Batman. What do you think I told them?).

Why am I prattling on about this? Well, because I was struck by the similarities between the emotions felt during these incidents and their immediate aftermath and those felt as I was being told that my marriage was over that day in August 2014.

Surreal calm. Time slows and momentarily stands still. Adrenaline. Heart pounds. Breathing shallows. A rush of emotion floods through numbed limbs. Divergent paths appear ahead. The beaten, bloody remains of my life. I was robbed. I was fucking robbed!! How dare you?!?! What gives you the fucking right to intrude on MY life like this?!? Who the fuck do you think you are?!?

Helpless. Hopeless.

Anger, fear, denial, injustice, revenge, compassion, understanding, empathy, sorrow, anger, justice. Anger. Defeat. Emasculation.

Emotions ripping through me like a tornado, devastating, violating all in their wake. Hopes, dreams, stability, security, my imagined future and the future of my family.

Gone, taken. Mugged. Robbed.

Why? Seeking answers, seeking sense. Maybe I'll find it, maybe I won't. Maybe I will never understand the full truth, the full reasons. Maybe she doesn't know the full reasons herself knowing only that things couldn't continue, things had to change and the time had come to walk away, however hard that may have been.

Often answers aren't forthcoming in the short-term but distance, time and a broader perspective can and should be used to unwrap the layers of doubt and confusion and reveal answers to the questions that really matter: what can I learn from this? How did I contribute to the breakdown of my relationship? How can I take these lessons and use them to create the future that I want? That I deserve? If we are to avoid making the mistakes of the past we must recognise, accept and learn from them. Only then can we truly move forward.

EMBRACING THE UNKNOWN

No man is promised tomorrow
If it comes, it's without guarantee
That today will be better than yesterday
That you will wake beside me

The sun it always rises
But clouds can obscure its shine
Cold winds cut through its warming glow
With a chill that bites inside

Change is an ever-present constant
What is, becomes what was
Appreciate moments whilst they're here because
What is found can become what was lost

Embrace boldly life's uncertainty
Know that to fight it will hold you back
From opportunities hidden within the chaos
From moving forwards without looking back

Be resolute on the unknowing
And unknowable road ahead
Beautiful destinations await you
So calm the storm that's in your head

Let the turmoil that surrounds you
Be not your enemy, but a friend
That will lead you to a better place
Until you find it, it's not the end

The only certainty we'll get from life
The only guarantee, for sure
Is that it's what we make of it
And the power to change it lies with you

BECOMING STRANGERS

Stability. Security. Familiarity. Borrrrring... What about adventure? Excitement? New experiences? Aren't they the things that give life its rich flavour? Aren't they the things that we will look back on and remember with a smile? Those peak experiences, the thrill of the new, the taste of the unfamiliar.

Well, yes, but by their very nature these are fleeting and transitory, and whilst these things are memorable the truth is that everything in our lives, no matter how new and exciting once, becomes familiar and, if we're not careful, over-familiar. When going through divorce we have to face losing everything that was once familiar, everything that comprised the day to day foundations of our lives. There can be few things that are more daunting and scary than having to face that journey on your own. At this time we realise just how much those familiar routines and rituals have come to define who we are, and we must face the questions of who we really are now that we are cut adrift from those things that acted as our anchors.

Who am I? At once both a small question and one of the largest that we can ask (and never really answer). During divorce this is something that we are forced to ask ourselves by virtue of what we are no longer – 'us'. Us, the thing that formed such a large part of who we have been – in my case for nineteen years – is no more. We must face up to becoming strangers to each other as we look to the future knowing that the person that has been a constant by our side, is now walking in their own, different direction. With each day, with each communication, with each silence, with each argument, we grow further and further apart, as the ties that made us 'us' become ever looser.

In the early days after separation, after the initial numbness, shock and despair have begun to fade, we begin to discover new things about ourselves. We can rediscover aspects of ourselves that have, perhaps inevitably, changed in accommodating ourselves to a life shared with another. This time of discovery and rediscovery can be exciting, and viewed from a distance it can take on a strangely nostalgic hue as our inbuilt defences remind us of the thrill and excitement we felt at the start of our new journey whilst seeking to lock away the anger, pain and hurt that were also a regular feature of those days.

In hindsight I ran on adrenaline for many months after my separation, embarking on a new relationship, buying new clothes, going on holiday, buying a new home – running headlong into becoming the new me with a new life that would be better than the old one that I had lost. But there comes a time when the adrenaline stops, when the thrill of the new is replaced by the 'new normal', where the longing for those once ever-presents – stability, security, familiarity – becomes greater and greater. Never is this longing more pronounced than at Christmas, a time of routines and rituals built around the most important things that we have in our lives – our families and loved ones. Despite my many blessings I couldn't help but ache for what I missed, that someone special with whom new routines could be made, new memories of shared love and laughter being created and a new future being built on love and the hope of creating something special and lasting.

That day will come. In the meantime, by adapting to a life that I never anticipated, I was becoming a new me, shaped by the challenges and adversity that always offer the greatest opportunities for growth and prepare us to accept life's future gifts with greater appreciation and to hold on to happiness wherever we find it.

HOME

'There's no place like home.'

One of the most famous movie lines ever spoken; nowadays a well-worn cliché. When you no longer have a home, you gain a vivid insight into just how true this saying is. Another well-worn cliché,

'You don't know what you've got till it's gone.'

Indeed. Indeed.

I have always been conscious of the many ways in which I have been very fortunate, even blessed, in my life and I would often consciously remind myself of the fact. One of the things I was always grateful for was owning a warm, comfortable home for my family and me. Still, however much you are grateful for and truly appreciate what you have, it's impossible to understand the depth of just how much it means until it's gone. Loss gives new meaning to what we had and creates a yearning for the apparently simple pleasures that are no more.

When my wife and I first split, I left my home with a small bag of essentials and an empty bag of ideas as to what I was going to do next. First port of call was, of course, my parents. As I entered with the awful news that I had completed the family hat-trick of three broken marriages (within one year, but don't let that put any potential future Mrs Williams' off; we're quite the catch – form an orderly queue, ladies...) one of the first questions after the initial disbelief was, 'Where are you going to live?'

No. Idea.

To be fair, at that point I had no idea about pretty much anything, with shock doing the job that nature intended and numbing the brain and the senses to protect against the emotional trauma that it would one day need come to terms with (and share with the world; it's strange the roads down which life can take us...). Staying with my parents wasn't an option as one of my brothers had beaten me to it. The only option I could think of was one of my best and oldest friends who happened to live locally and live alone. At times like this it's true that you see both the worst and the best of life, and amongst the very best things that life has to offer is the love and support of family and friends. My friend was unhesitating in offering me his spare room for as long as needed. I will be forever grateful to him for this, not only for providing the practical necessity of a roof over my head, but the wise counsel, sympathetic ear and welcome distractions that he offered throughout the four months that I inhabited the spare room. And also for the vacant look that accompanied my question about any house rules.

When your marriage has caved in, it's hard to think that you have fallen on your feet, but I certainly wasn't having to rebuild from rock bottom and that was a very welcome blessing. Those four months passed in a blur of a new relationship, new clothes, a fortieth birthday and the unravelling of a marriage and a family. And whilst the loss of a wife and a great deal of time with my children was predictably difficult – after all, having to face these things is something you never wish to contemplate – I hadn't anticipated how losing my home would affect me.

Going back and forth to my old home to pick up and drop off the children was a strange experience, and with each visit it became more and more apparent that home was no longer a concept that applied in my life. The stages along the way to detaching were odd, dictated by a growing sense of unease at being at my former home: from knocking on the door and walking in; to knocking and waiting at the door to be let in, to knocking at the door and waiting outside, no longer feeling comfortable setting foot into what was once my own little place in this big wide world. Over the weeks and months that followed my leaving, it was hard seeing my home become more and more not home, seeing the symbols of our shared life together being gradually removed and replaced until no sign of me remained and my home was no longer. This loss created a void, not just the obvious void of a place to call my own, but also in a missing sense of security and stability, a missing sense of having a place of my own in the world, and a missing sense of having somewhere that could offer stability for my children as we started to build a new life together as a different family unit. And it's funny what your mind – or mine at least – latches onto as a symbol of your loss.

My armchair.

Relaxing in my armchair, reading a good book, enjoying a cup of tea, listening to my children playing, all with a cat lying on the cushion behind me. That was my place. That was me.

DOWN AT THE END
OF LONELY STREET

'Write about something that scares you.'

After around six months of writing, a new friend – a writer – gave me this advice to help me to develop my own writing and to push myself into new places. Hmmm, there might be one slight problem with that: what the hell could I be scared to write about? Since beginning my blog, I had written candidly about my depression, feeling suicidal, my children living with another man, close encounters with sex people…

I racked my brains for ideas of what might scare me: sitting alone in my kitchen at the laptop I pondered; lying alone in my bed I considered; relaxing alone in my living room I debated with myself, eating alone in the silence of an empty house I dwelled. Alone with my thoughts; alone, searching for my fears. Alone. I realised, 'I am living what scares me. I am living my fears: I am living alone.' Okay, it wasn't strictly true, my children live with me half of the time; but there is still a sense of loneliness apparent in the role of single parent, where the everyday demands you once faced as a team you now have to face on your own.

I always liked being on my own. I like my own company and can think of many a worse way to while away the hours than burying my head in a good book, enjoying a cup of tea and watching the world go by. I have spent many an hour doing just that, and would often look forward to and savour such opportunities, those chances to escape from the busyness and repeated demands of everyday life. But these moments take on a different meaning when they cease to become moments, when they cease to become an escape from everyday life and instead become everyday life. When being alone is no longer a choice that we make, but a fear we must face.

When loneliness makes our acquaintance, it can take an almost physical form, of absence coming disguised as a heavy presence that we can feel beside us. A presence reminding us of our solitude, demanding to know why, in a world of seven billion people, not one of them is with us.

We live in an ever more individualistic age, an age where everything from consumerism to modern spirituality is geared towards self-actualisation, towards claiming what we rightfully deserve, because we're worth it. Where independence and strength are found in not needing anybody else but in marching to the beat of our own drum, where the rest of the world can accept us as we are, on our own terms. An age where we ain't changing for nobody, mister, where what you see is what you get and if you don't like it then you know what you can go and do, don't you?

In our age of self, here's what I was scared to say: I get lonely.

I'd like to think I've been reasonably successful in my life: I love my job, I am strong, I am confident; I have close lifelong friends; I have wonderful children, and I have a home. I can go anywhere and do anything, I can go where I want to, when I want to, with who I want to. I am comfortable enough in my own skin to lay myself bare for all to see – and judge – as I seek to better understand myself, hoping that in the process I am helping others that wish to do the same. Yet it scares me to admit that I get lonely. That I am lonely.

As my fingers type out the words 'I am lonely', my mind seeks justification and prepares the case for the defence. 'I am not looking for sympathy', 'I don't want you to think that I'm some sort of sadsack', 'I'm not sat here crying into my Weetabix...'

(really, I'm not). Because it is hard to write 'I am lonely' without a sense that it translates to 'I am needy, I am weak'. I am not. Here's what I am: human.

We all crave connection, it is a core part of the human condition and we are by design pack creatures, social animals. We are products of our environment and our identity is formed in large part through our relations with others. As we journey through life, our character is both developed and revealed in the roles that we adopt: son, daughter; brother, sister; friend, enemy; father, mother. Husband, wife. We are one of the few species that create lifelong partnerships and this expectation of how life should be is threaded through the very fabric of our society. When your lifelong partnership is terminated and you find you are alone, it is hard not to feel that something, someone, is missing.

I have met some wonderful people since I have been single, and I'm fortunate to live in an age where I have been able to virtually meet many more. We are able to connect and communicate with others more easily than we ever have before. But when the message alerts are quiet, when the notifications stop, the silence rings and reminds me of what I miss. Someone special. Their smile. Their laugh. Their embrace. The hundreds of little things that add up to the biggest thing – that one person that will always be there, no matter what. Someone to laugh with, to make plans with, to dream with and to share my inner self with. Someone to unlock parts of me that otherwise lie dormant, to whom I can offer the gifts of my best self.

I don't need another half – the last time I checked I was pretty whole as I am (more whole than I would like to be in fact, but that's middle-age for you). I don't need anyone to fill a gap inside of me. I don't need anyone to help fill my time, and I won't accept 'anyone' in an attempt to lock the door to keep loneliness at bay. Because loneliness hurts, but settling for less than you deserve hurts even more.

DISCONNECTED

Disconnected
Cut loose from life
Conversation, laughter
All around me
Passing me by
Alone
Isolated from the world without
A floating island
In a foreign sea

LESSONS FROM A RECOVERING REJECT

Have you ever been rejected? Of course you have. We all have. And doesn't it just hurt like a...? I'll let you insert your own expletive. I'm not going to whine on about it, I'm not the first and I won't be the last. But no matter how many times it's happened to us, no matter that we know that in time we'll get over it, no matter how we try to distract ourselves... it still hurts like hell. So I'll go ahead and presume that we can all agree – rejection sucks. And no rejection that I've experienced sucks quite as bad as the rejection of divorce.

Not only is divorce a personal rejection – which is bad enough – it is the rejection of the shared promise that life held for you as you set out on the journey of marriage. Most painfully, it is the rejection of the family that you have built together. Many times in the year following my break up – as I adapted to my new life, as I struggled through the heartache of divorce, as I learned to live as a single dad getting used to spending half of my life away from my children – a nagging thought chipped its way to the forefront of my consciousness: this life was a choice. Only the choice wasn't mine.

The pain, the heartache, the arguments, the tears, the fear, the worry, the loneliness – this was considered to be the better path. This was preferable to staying married. It doesn't leave you feeling too great, let me tell you. And such thoughts can cause your sense of self-worth to take quite a battering, if you let them. So, what can you do about it? Well, if you want to get through it here's what you're not going to do: you're not going to wallow in self-pity. Of course you will feel sorry for yourself, perhaps deservedly so; and yes, you will hurt, you will feel miserable, you will cry and question why the hell it had to happen. That's okay, that's normal, and feeling that and not trying to deny it is healthy. But staying there, making it your default setting – not good. Yes, somebody has hurt you, and yes, you may be on the canvas, but the last thing you want is to be the person that is responsible for tolling the ten count over your crumpled figure.

What if you were felled by a punch below the belt? What if it just wasn't fair? What if you just can't move forward until you understand how the rules could have been flouted so brazenly, so hurtfully? What about closure dammit?!? It doesn't matter. It doesn't matter. It doesn't matter. Your relationship stubbed out like a half-smoked cigarette; you, discarded like the empty packet. Closure? You've got to find it in yourself. Whoever it was that put you on the floor, how they did it, why they did it… it's up to you to get yourself up again. And it's probably best to assume that the person that put you there isn't going to be the one that's holding out a hand to help you.

There are always lessons to be learned; lessons about ourselves, our partners, our expectations, our boundaries. Lessons about our hopes, our fears, our mistakes and our virtues. Lessons about our worth. About our self-worth. We can become better, wiser people in taking responsibility for our failings, in apologising and making amends where we can, in taking an honest look at ourselves and our role in our break-ups. But in so doing we also need to remember that we are imperfect creatures and our failings, our mistakes, should not be used as sticks to beat ourselves with and to further batter our tenderised self-worth. Instead we should consider them to be guides that will help us to write better stories in the future. Maybe sometimes we need to just accept that those that hurt and reject us are imperfect too. That they, like us, are just doing their best to find happiness in this sometimes messy, confusing world.

If you have been rejected, if you feel about as desirable as a Betamax video recorder or a Sinclair ZX Spectrum, remember that millions of people loved them once. Hell, even Skoda became popular. So, lick your wounds, learn your lessons and don't give up; for one day you will find your happy ending.

TIME, ALWAYS TIME

Post-break up I found myself listening to too much Damien Rice. A particular lyric played on a loop in my mind, from the song 'Older Chests', extolling the age-old remedy for the broken heart: time.

You don't expect to be broken-hearted in your forties, and you certainly don't expect it to happen twice in a year. Isn't that stuff for teenagers? Like any pain, when it's at its most intense we would give anything for it to stop. We can distract ourselves for a time but it's always there and it is scant consolation that deep down we know that there is a medicine, one true cure that will heal the broken pieces: always time.

There is no fast forward (or rewind), however much we may wish to accelerate (or avoid) the grieving process. But sometimes we do things that slow our progress. One of the ways we do this is with three small words: let's stay friends. By staying friends we initially shield ourselves from the worst of the pain, placing a band-aid over our wounds. In the familiarity of each other's company, we conduct a careful dance, trying to shield each other and ourselves from the pain that we know lurks underneath, whilst trying to find a gentler way to move on with a minimum of hurt. But the pain can't be smoothed away and it can't be avoided, it will distribute itself gradually over time until something causes it to grab you by the guts, forcing you to face it and to deal with it. Most likely this will happen when someone new enters the picture, when your friendship is forced to take a back seat and your special place is reserved for another, carrying with them the hopes that were once to be found within you. And the pain won't be denied any longer.

Time, always time. It must be allowed to do its work to replace pain with acceptance, and regrets with hope for a better future. But to allow this, for things to work out fine – according to Guns N Roses at least – we need something else too, patience. Patience is indeed a virtue but it is a difficult one to apply, particularly in the fast-paced world in which we live where such store is set in immediacy and short-term wish fulfilment. And what we need here is trust. Trust that the future does indeed hold better days, and in moving towards them we can patiently use our time to learn the lessons that are available to help us to understand why love wasn't enough, and what we can do differently in the future to avoid the mistakes of the past.

Another song that struck a chord with me in the immediate aftermath of separation was 'The Masterplan' by Oasis, in which Noel Gallagher sings beautifully of the need to sail our words away, with acquiesce and with hope. When relationships break down it is easy to be filled with regrets, to think about the words that we could have said and the things that we could have done differently. At times amidst the raw pain of separation, regrets can be all that we seem to have, and we can scramble around frantically in our minds looking for the things that we can say or do now to make a difference, words and deeds that could somehow turn back the tide and make things right. We can be torn between thoughts, to fight or to accept, to hold on or to let go, to keep in touch or to break away completely. There are no firm rights or wrongs, we can only do our best amongst the rising tide of our emotions to ride the wave that feels best at that time, especially when we know the journey will be difficult whichever choice we make.

Having made difficult decisions, it is inevitable that we shall look back and question the wisdom of our choices, and at times to allow regrets to seep in and to infect our thoughts. How we act in these turbulent times is one of the challenges that we must face on our way to what we hope will be a better future. Because in the end we need to be able to look ourselves in the mirror, to be able to walk tall with our dignity and self-respect intact. There are things we may need to say and do to bring closure, one way or the other. And when we do so, amidst our hurt and confusion we must strive to be true to our higher principles, to follow the course that feels right in our heart, with sincere intent, without fear, and without wishing to cause hurt to others.

In saying what we need to say, we leave ourselves emotionally raw, swaying between the hope that things can be different and the fear of facing what we have lost and having to accept that we will have to find a way to move on and let go. But in being true to ourselves when we act, in acting out of love and not fear, in being prepared to accept whatever outcome knowing that whatever happens we did our best, then we will find our peace and one way or another we will move on to what life has in store for us next.

Sometimes our best isn't enough to get us what we want, and at those times acceptance can be difficult to come by. But find it we must, because as long as we are true to ourselves we will always be moving towards a better future.

HOPE

Hold on to the faintest of glimmers and know,
that this dark winter is

Only but a season, and though it may be cold and dark, I

Promise you, that

Everything is going to be alright, your light will shine again

SINGLE PARENTHOOD FOR BEGINNERS

'Daddy.'

There is no sweeter sound in the world than the word Daddy from the mouths of your children. Of course there are also times when its sound is rather less than sweet – 'Daddy, that's not fair!', 'Daddy, I'm finished, can you come and wipe, I think it's a messy one…' – but for my purposes here let's stick with the sweetness. And from sweetness let's jump to the bitterest pill that you are forced to swallow when your marriage collapses – you will no longer be spending every day with your children. You will wake up and they won't be there. You will arrive home from work without them to greet you. You will go to bed at night without being able to check in on them and kiss their foreheads. These realisations are sudden and devastating. They are accompanied by fear over how their lives will be affected and a crushing sense of failure that your children, the most precious people in your world, will no longer have a stable, loving home with their mummy and daddy.

Then comes the heart-wrenching, inevitable realisation of a new truth: that sooner or later another man will become a significant person in the lives of your children. Nothing can prepare you for this hurt, pain and sense of powerlessness. And so you set about doing what you can to create a new life for them, new routines, always making sure that they know that you love them and are there for them even when you're not there physically.

Looking back from a distance this period of adjustment seems like a blur, a foggy period of transition from everything that was stable and secure to a new world of doubts and just doing my best. A new world of visits to familiar places with a new and unfamiliar definition of family, akin to a body that is missing a limb and must learn to adapt and function in a new way.

One of the things that you realise – and is frequently pointed out to you – is that this situation isn't unusual anymore. Of course that is scant consolation – everybody wants what is best for their own children and being a 'broken' family (or a 'different' family) never figured in my vision of the future. A source of real sadness for me was the realisation that, as my children were young at the time of my divorce, they will grow up with little or no memory of our complete family despite the fact that my ex-wife and I were together for nineteen years. But then many children have to grow up with all-too vivid and painful memories of their parents' divorce. There is always a silver-lining of sorts to be found, I guess.

Without the counterbalance of a wife to raise your children alongside you, you can become all too aware of your personal deficiencies. As a man with a daughter, I am now acutely aware that I am pretty useless when it comes to doing her hair, and deficiencies in my organisational skills in the home, though improving, are frequently thrown into sharp focus: when getting everything ready for school in the morning; when trying to keep on top of homework (for under five year olds, don't get me started on that subject), for making sure there are enough clean school uniforms when every day a white polo shirt comes home covered in paint and ink… Somehow though you manage, and as in everything you just do your best.

Even though you know that is all that you can do, and even though you know that the most important things that you can give to your children are your time and attention – and even though I am one of the fortunate fathers that has shared custody of the children – there is a little part of you that questions yourself, that wonders whether your children prefer the life that they have with your ex. For the children, shared parenting in two different homes becomes the norm, and although any reasonable, mature consideration of the situation concludes that this is not a competition between parents, in the inevitable moments of doubt and loneliness the niggling question arises. And then the time comes when another man enters their lives.

As hard as it is to face losing your wife and the thought that she will, sooner or later, love another, somewhere underneath it all is the awareness that so too will you. But nothing can really prepare you for another man entering the lives of your children. For the thought that no matter how good a father you can be, no matter how special and unique and wonderful your relationship with your children is, there is somebody else that will become a significant influence in their lives. If I'm honest there are times when I'm not sure I will ever really come to terms with this. You get on with it – after all, what choice do you have? – but it leaves its mark on you, on the dreams that you had for your future, and on the anticipation of the special family events that you looked forward to when you embarked on the wonderful and scary world of parenthood – birthdays, graduations, weddings, grandchildren – suddenly there is a new and unwanted presence in the storybook of their lives.

I've worked hard on greater acceptance; I strongly believe that if we are to truly make the most of the limited time that we have on this earth we need to accept the world as it is and not how we thought or wished it should be. There is a saying that it is not the strongest that survives but the most adaptable to change and I guess that is true of families; through adversity we can learn how fantastically adaptable people can be to their circumstances and there is no one certain way to raise a happy, secure, loving family. But adapting to a new definition of family isn't easy and it isn't quick, and for me a sense of stability is something that took a long time to find. Sometimes I still doubt that I have. But when I'm with my children we still smile, we still laugh, and together we are creating many happy new memories.

Above all we know that we will love and be there for each other. Always.

THE GREATEST OF FRIENDS?

We frequently read of the apparently idyllic marriages of celebrities biting the dust. Following the announcement that Gary Lineker's marriage had ended, the Match Of The Day presenter insisted that he and his ex-wife remained, 'very close and the greatest of friends'. I sincerely hoped this to be true. Divorce can be a brutal process that I wouldn't wish upon anyone and if from the wreckage of broken promises and dreams a genuine friendship can be salvaged, then that is to be respected, applauded even. So why did I feel so cynical?

I count myself among those whose first reaction to those words was something along the lines of, 'yeah, right, course you are'. After pause for reflection I felt a little crappy at taking such a dim and condescending view of the statement. I do believe that people can be friends after divorce and there are plenty of examples to attest to this. So what was my problem? Well, I wasn't in that place, and for the near three years since separation I have been a very long way from 'the greatest of friends'. Will I ever get there? Honestly, I don't know.

On first separating, it is difficult to conceive of the possibility that the person you have shared so much with for so long will fade out of your life, or worse, become an enemy. Of course you are aware of what divorce can do to people, how appallingly people that once swore to love, honour and cherish each other until death do they part can treat each other.

But that won't happen to you, will it? You're above that, and nothing can take away all that you have shared. And anyway, you know each other, really know each other; whatever happens you will be dignified, you will be civil. You're good people. I thought so too. As hard as it was to hear, I could accept the reasons for our separation and, with time, came to terms with the fact that the rest of our lives were to be spent apart from each other. I came to truly believe that in the long run I would find greater happiness than any I had known before. Yes, the dust would settle, we'd adapt to our new circumstances and build lives of our own. We would share 100% commitment to doing what was best for our children and, in time, we would be friends. Well let me tell you, it ain't easy…

A few weeks after the revelation of the final demise of our marriage, and in the early stages of recovery from that savage blow to the guts, I told those around me that I held no grudges, that we would divorce amicably and yes, in time we would be friends. Sadly in today's society, divorce has touched many families and I came to face many knowing looks and sympathetic, but not utterly convincing, nods of heads. 'If I had a pound for every time I'd heard that…'

I took advantage of the free legal advice that I was entitled to – discovering that it was free for a reason – before selecting a solicitor to act on my behalf in the divorce, which I was keen to finalise as soon as I could. For right or wrong, I'm not comfortable with the anticipation of known troubles ahead, my attitude to dealing with such situations is pretty much akin to pulling off a plaster – do it quickly and get the pain out of the way. But really it doesn't work like that. For me, being divorced was important symbolically in helping me to move on and accept that the marriage was over, but the feelings that surround it don't follow any externally imposed timetable. In dealing with the powerful and painful emotions and rituals of divorce, the idea of a present or future friendship slipped further and further away.

It is odd to enlist a professional stranger to act on your behalf 'against' the person that you thought you would be spending the rest of your life with. But there is no getting away from the fact that divorce is an adversarial process and throughout it our thoughts turn from 'we' to 'me'. What is best for me and for my future? Recognising this attitude in your ex is painful and difficult not to take personally, proof as it is that you no longer matter in the way that you once did, that their plans for the future no longer concern you and what is best for your future. Because now that is solely your responsibility. And in the case of a mother or father, that responsibility is not just to you but to your children too. In the confused, unfamiliar emotional terrain of marital breakdown, professional legal support – detached, practical and logical support – can be essential.

As divorces go I would say mine was one of the 'better' ones, not exactly a 'conscious uncoupling' (ughhh) but no 'War Of The Roses' either. The major issues that can make divorce so painful and that can set out the stall for years of battles and recriminations – child custody and money – were settled quickly and with little conflict. But friendship was, and remains, elusive. Why is this? And does it point to some flaw in me? I'd like to think I'm a good person and can honestly say that I wouldn't do anything to deliberately hurt anybody. That's not to say that my actions haven't caused hurt to others, but I do my best to treat others how I would hope that they would treat me. And as such I would have thought that future friendship would be possible for me. But in the end there is no rulebook in the complex and often messy world of human relationships.

Some people grow closer after divorce, others develop a lifelong bitterness and enmity. I've never wanted to live with anger and bitterness, recognising how they could consequently poison other significant relationships in my life and damage my happiness and health in the process. But in contemplating and dealing with what you have lost, it is perhaps inevitable for most that anger and bitterness will have to be faced and tackled. I carried that anger and bitterness and at times it got the better of me, but it has passed. Still, the seeds of friendship have yet to sprout.

When a marriage ends, it is rarely a truly mutual decision. Even if both parties can recognise the need to go their separate ways, it will usually be one person that has instigated the start of that journey. It is unlikely that the decision will have been taken quickly. As such, one party will have a head start in the processing of the emotions of divorce, and in anticipating and preparing mentally for a different future to the one that was for so long taken for granted. Being at such different stages of the grieving process can make it difficult for each to comprehend the behaviours of the other, and as you begin to become strangers, friendship can become a distant goal.

I have found that in becoming strangers and in establishing separate lives, we are given the space to heal, to move on and to live in a different present. In doing so, over time maybe the door to some sort of future friendship can open. But divorce leaves a scar and I'm not sure that it ever fully heals. I guess the ability to live with that scar, to wear it as a sign of the adversity that we have faced and overcome rather than as an ugly sign of failure, is part of what will determine whether friendship is possible.

For now I am living for me and for my children. And, hopefully, the lessons that I have learned will help to build a strong foundation for a future relationship that will last the course; a relationship where we will grow closer together with the passing of the years rather than grow apart. I'm not perfect. I've made mistakes. But I can look myself in the mirror and be comfortable with how I have dealt with my divorce. I can look my children in the eyes and tell them that I did my best and I never compromised my values. And nothing is more important than that.

A LIFE SEGMENTED

When I was eight, I fell off my bike and dislocated my elbow. It bloody knacked. The pain wasn't helped by the friendly doctor in Accident & Emergency who helpfully advised me that 'crying isn't going to help'. Yeah thanks, wish I'd thought of that.

It was months before my arm would fully straighten and, although it hasn't caused any long term problems, it's always felt… different. Not in any way that I can explain, not in terms of any tangible feeling, just different. It could be a psychological thing, I guess, or it might just be that we have a natural sense of our right arm feeling different to the left. Who knows? Anyway, what's the point of that random bit of rambling? One word: dislocation.

'Dislocation: disturbance from a proper, original,
or usual place or state.'

This, ladies and gentleman, is how life has felt to me post-divorce; dislocated. And I'm not sure when, or even if, it will be fully straightened. So much of the last few years has been spent adjusting: to being a single parent, to being single, to living alone, to dating (and then not dating, then dating, then not dating); to being a different person to who I was before, cut loose from the conventions of marriage to navigate a foreign landscape, without a map. So many things to try and make sense of, so many circumstances in which a new definition of self is needed, a self untethered from familiar roles and routines and guided by the compass of one's own instincts. For better or for worse.

Prior to divorce, my anchor point, my point of stability, had always been my family. That's not to say life was all happy clappy (well, obviously, I suffered with depression and ended up getting divorced), but there was a sense of wholeness about my life. And now, well, now there isn't. That's not to say I don't appreciate what I have in my life – I truly do know how fortunate I am to have family, friends, a lovely home, a great job – but life feels very different these days. My life has lost that sense of wholeness and instead it feels segmented.

One of the recommendations for a psychologically healthy life is to not put all of your eggs in one basket, to focus on developing and maximising various aspects of your life so that if there are difficulties in one area, there are plenty of other areas from which meaning and satisfaction are gained. One of the reasons ex-athletes often struggle to cope with retirement is that the single-minded and necessarily selfish pursuit of achieving goals in one aspect of life – essential if one is to reach the summit of one's sport – is not conducive to functioning healthily within the 'normal' world inhabited by the ex-athlete. Like I say, I'm very fortunate to have various 'segments' to my life that are hugely gratifying to me and provide a real sense of purpose and meaning but it's difficult to shake that sense of dislocation, of a segmented life lacking in structure and cohesiveness.

I expect that many will wonder what the hell I'm going on about – if I'm honest, I'm not really sure myself – but I know that that sense is there and when I've mentioned it to others in a similar situation they have identified with it too. Still, I'm finding it very difficult to articulate. I know that deep down I hope to find that sense of wholeness, that feeling that things are as they ought to be and that life feels settled again. Don't get me wrong, life has taken on a spontaneity this year that has at times been exciting, but the thrill of a rollercoaster lies in the brevity of its twists and turns, after a while you start to feel sick from lurching in every direction and you want it to stop.

Will I find a sense of wholeness? I'm not sure. I could be all deep and profound and talk of a future shift within myself that allows me to feel settled and at peace regardless of whatever chaos may surround me. I would love to think that could happen but I can't honestly say I expect it anytime soon. Ultimately my anchor – my family – has taken on a shape that I never expected nor wanted and it will never be whole in the sense that it was. I guess I have accepted that to a point but the truth remains that it still doesn't feel 'right' to me that half of my life is spent away from my children, that half of their lives are spent away from me.

That's my normal now, but normal will never be what the majority of my life has been spent believing it to be. Life's good, but it's not right.

10 THINGS TO EXPECT
WHEN YOUR MARRIAGE ENDS

You know what really sucks balls? Getting divorced. Big time. But three years on from the end of my marriage I've learned a lot and I'd like to share some of the key lessons in the hope that they may help other men – and women – going through the turbulence of a broken marriage. So without further ado, let class commence.

1. Who the hell are you?
Remember your wedding day? Best day of your life, right? A day shared with the most special person in your life, your wife. Remember her? Be prepared to wonder where the hell she went. The journey from life-partners and soul mates to warring adversaries can be alarmingly quick and can leave you shell-shocked. Divorce is, by its nature, an adversarial process and despite best intentions, the changed focus from 'we' to 'me' quickly creates a distance from which your now ex-partner can become barely recognisable.

2. Who the hell am I?
If you have been part of a couple for any length of time, chances are you will have made compromises, compromises that enabled you to live as a couple and to respect each other's differences. Upon separating you will find yourself rediscovering old parts of yourself and also discovering new parts. These discoveries can

be exciting, intoxicating even, but can also lead you – and those around you – to wonder who you are now that you are no longer defined by the role of husband.

3. She's going to sleep with other men
I can't speak for the women here but I'd place a large wager that for 99% of men a predominant, sickening fear in the wake of marriage breakdown is that their loved one will, sooner or later, be in the arms – and the bed – of another man. And fuck me, can that drive you mad. What can I say? It's going to happen. It's going to hurt. And there's nothing you can do about it. Well, you could shout, scream, cry, beg and make an all-round arse of yourself but I'd recommend you don't. Believe me, your future self will thank me. And anyway…

4. You're going to sleep with other women
Now we're talking! Free at last, free at last, thank God Almighty you're free at last! Free to get yourself back out there and have some new X-rated adventures. It is undeniably exciting to realise that, having chosen to spend the rest of your life sleeping with only one person (I hope), there are at least one or two other women out there that are going to let you do rude things with them. Things could be worse.

5. You've just got to feel it
Marriage breakdown and divorce hurts. Like, really hurts. Hurts. Like. Hell. Love, security, home, family life, friends, stability, money, comfort, the future – all can be lost in the wake of divorce and all will be affected to a greater or lesser extent. So, it's going to hurt. Why bother pointing out the bloody obvious, Matthew? Because we don't like people to know we're hurt, do we? Especially us blokes. Often we don't even want to admit it to ourselves. We are from the land of the stiff upper lip, of stoicism in the face of setbacks, a land where we pull ourselves up by the bootstraps and get on with it. But there's no getting away from it, it's going to fucking hurt and you'd better accept that and you'd

better let yourself feel it. Cry, shout, scream, hit a punchbag as hard as you can, whatever it takes to really feel it. We might want to run from our feelings but we can't hide. They're there, and one way or another, some day, some way they are going to let you know about it, no matter how hard you try to fight against it.

Getting pissed, getting laid, getting away – these can help you through the acute phase and numb the pain but they won't take it away. Unless you allow yourself to face the pain and feel it, you'll never be free of it.

6. You have no idea...

Divorce is a minefield, and potentially a bloody expensive one at that. Do your homework. Read articles, get legal advice as soon as possible and talk to people that have been there – and believe them. Of course, everyone's experience is different and one person's tale of hell doesn't have to be a portent of things to come. But... it's going to be tough and there's no escaping the fact. However amicable, however reasonable, divorce is traumatic. Accept this, but also know that you'll get through it and one day it will be but a painful memory, and one that may well lay the foundations of future happiness.

7. You'll be so lonely

Loneliness, bone-aching loneliness, will make your acquaintance, both the physical loneliness of being on your own and the emotional loneliness of being alone. As the saying goes, nature abhors a vacuum and the new space in your life will need to be filled. The natural tendency may be to fill it with somebody else but this isn't necessarily the best option, particularly if you are dealing (or not) with the emotions of your break up and/or you don't really know what you want other than to not feel lonely.

8. You're free, to do what you want to do

There are other ways to tackle loneliness. Being newly single is an opportunity to travel, make new friends, spend time with old friends, pick up an interest that you've lost along the way or discover new things that alight your passions and offer the opportunity to meet and connect with new people. The internet places a world of opportunity at your fingertips – activities to try, people to meet, groups to join – if you're going to be single, it couldn't happen at a better time.

It's not often we are able to do what we want to do and live how we want to live without having to consider the wishes of someone else. You don't know how long this opportunity will last; make the most of it.

9. Really, you have no idea...

Dating, bloody hell. If you are emerging from a long relationship, be prepared to be dazzled. Modern dating for those of us who are new to it all can be bewildering, bizarre and bloody brilliant, sometimes all at the same time. Tinder, texting, swinging and sexting, searching and settling – the options are limitless. It can be great fun but it can also be disappointing and dispiriting.

Try not to have too many expectations, accept it will probably take a while to find someone special – if that's what you're looking for – take things as they come and enjoy it. You may need to develop a thick skin as you ride the dating rollercoaster but use it as an opportunity to meet new people and to meet the new you, to discover what it is you really want. But please, do it with decency; if you find yourself dating in your thirties and forties, chances are you've been through some shit and so have the people you're going to be dating. Have some respect for that and don't mess people about.

10. Most importantly, remember...

You're going to be alright.

PART 2

BATTLING THE BLACK DOG: DEPRESSION

I HAD A BLACK DOG

As I faced up to divorce and its attendant changes and stresses, a dark spectre lurked on the fringes of my consciousness. Winston Churchill used the metaphor of the black dog to describe his bouts of depression and – in the only sentence I will ever be mentioned alongside Winston Churchill – I too am the owner of a black dog. It wasn't my intention to be a mental health advocate when I began writing. In my early blog posts I referred to my previous struggles with depression, and the resulting feedback from others that were struggling prompted me to want to tackle the subject head-on. In reality, if I was to share my journey truthfully I couldn't not tackle it.

I have always sought to be open about my struggles; I like to try and find the positives in the challenges that I face in my life and being an open person by nature I felt something of a responsibility to try and help others by challenging the stigma and misunderstanding that exists around the illness. And make no mistake, depression is an illness.

At its worst, it is an all-consuming, torturous, desperate, lonely, terrifying illness that has the power to strip you of your very sense of self, to crush your self-worth and your dignity as you try and fail to face the obstacles, both real and those that are perceived in your damaged mind, of everyday life. Depression closes around you like a prison and from within its walls it is all but impossible to conceive of a way to escape. You are no longer you, and it is incredibly difficult to comprehend just who and what it is that depression has turned you into.

At its most severe, depression offers not a single moment of respite from its cruel grip, the physical sensation of your head trapped in a vice with a storm of terrifying thoughts constantly battering your mind, shaking, sweating, losing the ability to think and speak coherently, and the ability to spontaneously smile and laugh cut from your being as if by a surgeon. This suffering can persist, unrelenting, for months, and in some people for years. And so, exhausted, the only haven appears to be beneath the covers, where we find one final cruelty as our ability to sleep is lost.

There is no exaggeration here. And whilst it is impossible to conceive of unless you have experienced it, by writing about it I have always hoped that more people can at least open their minds to the idea that depression is a real and serious illness. The sense of disconnection from others and, critically, from yourself makes depression a cruelly isolating experience and as such the words of others who understand and who have prevailed over the illness can be a huge source of comfort and support when these are in desperately short supply.

They can also help those that are around the sufferer to better understand what they are going through. The sufferer's pain can be compounded by the sense that they are somehow to blame for their illness, that some failing or weakness on their part caused it and that their continuing condition is their fault for not being stronger or more resilient. It must be said that being around somebody in the grip of depression is a draining, isolating and emotionally exhausting experience itself and relationships can be rocked to their foundations. Families and friends do their best but whilst they can visit the sufferer in their prison, they can't break down the walls, they can't provide the key. Only the sufferer themselves can do that, but the love, support and care of others, including qualified professionals, are an essential part of the cure. And when the depression passes, the bonds of love and friendship can be stronger than ever before.

Therein lies an important truth of depression, it passes. There is no magic solution, no immediate fix, but a gradual process of recovery facilitated by a combination of things that together help to lift the sufferer out of despair and into the brightness of new days of hope. And there are truly no brighter days than those that follow the darkness of depression.

It is difficult to accept that a black dog lies within. Following my first depression I managed to convince myself that it was a one-off event and that in my recovery lay the proof that I had conquered whatever it was that had caused it to strike. I had to reassess that view when it returned to viciously shake me from my complacency. Now I try to maintain a balanced view of myself as someone that has the seeds of depression within, whilst not accepting as inevitable the possibility of a future episode.

Vigilance is key. We need to understand depression – as far as it is possible to understand an illness whose roots are still largely unknown – and understand ourselves, our triggers, and the sometimes subtle behavioural signs that indicate that the black dog may have started padding along in our slipstream. It's important to keep busy, take one day at a time, and be around others, whilst recognising that sometimes it is necessary to take time out to rest. And always to know that 'this too shall pass'.

Depression can be very difficult to admit to but I don't fear being thought weak for admitting my struggles, because I know from experience just how much strength it takes to overcome them.

THE PROMISE OF DAY

Tear off my skin, climb outside
To escape the captors that imprison my mind
Depart the body, broken and used
Dragging my demons, to my soul they fuse

Extinguishing hope, narrowing view
Life as I'd known it, over, through
The life that's coming, distant, unclear
Suffocating, breathless, blanketed in fear

A void widens afore me
The abyss, it calls my name
Hell affords its invite
Another broken soul to claim

As swirling madness batters
All that once was good
My silent scream, echoes
Throughout an empty wood

Stripped of all that held me
Raw flesh angrily exposed
Liberating loneliness
It's me and me alone

Descending through the darkness
Weighted by my blackened soul
Praying I find rock bottom
It's my only chance to grow

I will endure the torture
From the ashes I shall stride
In the light of a new morning
I will see with brand new eyes

Scars no longer angry
Mere patterns of the past
Wisdom sealed within them
To guide along the path

The sun it always rises
Shadows never stay
Persevere through the darkness
Night holds the promise of day

I'M NOT OKAY (& THAT'S OKAY)

'Hi, how are you?'
'Yeah, I'm alright thanks, are you?
Well, no actually I'm not, I'm not okay.'

I'm not okay. Three small words, three of the biggest words you can ever say out loud. Yet, to so many people – and especially men – these words are almost impossible to say. Some people retreat ever further into themselves, others overcompensate by being overly cheerful as they try to maintain the illusion that they are fine.

No matter who surrounds us – friends, colleagues, loved ones – sometimes we feel all alone and all we want is for one person, just one, to take us aside and ask, 'Are you okay?' The conversation that opens this chapter was the first conversation I had with my doctor as I slid into my first crippling depression. It was April 2006 and the black dog had been following me for around three months, and things were getting worse to the point that it was seriously affecting my ability to function in daily life. My grip was loosening day by day as my mental health deteriorated and it was becoming more and more apparent to me that this wasn't just going to go away.

It was only at this point that I began to realise that what was happening to me was an illness; it was something that was happening to me, not something that I was doing to myself by 'being miserable' or failing to 'cheer up'. I was suffering with clinical depression.

Since that first horrific episode, I suffered a major relapse in 2013 that lasted four months. Through these experiences I have learned to recognise the signs that things are not quite right with me; on their own these signs can seem pretty innocuous but if I have a number of them together and they last more than a few days then I know that I need to be more vigilant with and take better care of myself. These signs include:

• Lack of motivation
• Feeling tired all the time
• Waking early/disturbed sleep
• Withdrawing and wanting to be on my own
• Lack of spontaneous thought
• Loss of interest in things that I usually enjoy,
  especially listening to music
• Lack of patience and becoming snappy

This increased self-awareness is an important part of recovery and being able to recognise potential triggers helps me to guard against complacency and tells me, 'Hey, be careful; you're not okay, but you will be.'

Why is it so hard to admit that we are not okay, that we hurt, that we're struggling? Logically we know that everybody struggles at some time in their life, and yet when it's us, we worry about what people will think, we don't want to be thought of as 'weak' or to 'let people down'. Maybe we don't want to admit our 'weakness' to ourselves. Here's what I've learned: admitting that we're not okay takes strength. If doing so were weak then it wouldn't be so damned difficult. Confronting our fears, admitting that we need help – that takes strength and that is why it is often such a big step on the road to recovery, to taking some control over the situation and to dealing with it.

Will other people think we're weak? Maybe some will, but that speaks about them and not about us. We could all use help sometimes and during such times our priority should be in seeking it, in caring about what's best for us and not the opinions and prejudices of others. And wouldn't most of us want to be there for a friend or family member that needs us? At such times we really do see the best in people and we can really learn to appreciate the value with which others hold us.

Sometimes what we see as weakness is actually just a characteristic of who we are, free from judgements such as 'strong' or 'weak'. The very characteristics that hurt us may actually serve us well at other times, in other circumstances. We are all a mixture of weakness and strength, of resolve and vulnerability, and we will all face illness, heartbreak, grief, loss and confusion in our lives. The more willing we are to accept that then the more likely we are to be able to ask for help when we need it. This is important. As male suicide rates show, lives depend on it.

As even the former world heavyweight champion Tyson Fury admits that he needs help to deal with mental health problems maybe it's time to truly recognise that even the biggest and strongest amongst us can feel broken and damaged sometimes. Admitting you're not okay may be one of the hardest things you ever do; it is also one of the strongest.

WE NEED TO TALK ABOUT SUICIDE

Wait!! Come back!

Okay, so it isn't the most enticing chapter title ever and the first thing I ought to say is that no, I am not suicidal. Far from it. But in the past I have been, and I feel that I have something of value to say on the subject.

I have received a lot of comments regarding my writing, many praising me for being brave in sharing my thoughts and feelings, particularly around depression. Such feedback has always been a real pleasure to receive and it means a great deal to me, but to be honest, it never felt brave. Writing about suicide however is different. This is tough. This is uncomfortable. And that's why I feel that it is important that I write it.

One of the things that I have learned in recent years is that when faced with things that challenge us, things that we know will be tough, more often than not it is the difficult path that is the right one to take. And there are few subjects closer to my heart than this. I need to write this. So why is it so difficult for me to write about? Despite having written very openly about my struggles with depression, this feels different. I guess there may be something in the fact that, thankfully, depression is being talked about publicly much more these days with many high profile figures talking about their experiences. I'm in very good company here.

Maybe it is getting easier to speak about depression because, despite the stigma that still exists, there is a growing acceptance that it is indeed an illness, a serious illness that kills many people, especially young men. Maybe this leads to why suicide is still so difficult to speak about – depression kills, but how do we tell people that depression kills when ultimately a person that commits suicide is making a choice to end their own life? How can we say that depression killed them? If suicide is a choice it is natural that people that haven't known the turmoil of severe depression will question how that decision was made, especially given the terrible pain caused to those left behind and especially any children. That's just selfish. Isn't it?

Imagine. For a minute try to imagine just how bad things must be for the sufferer that he or she makes that ultimate choice. It goes against every instinct that we have. The strongest instinct that we have is overcome – that to survive. How does this happen? Perhaps the most harrowingly accurate description of the anguish of depression that I have read is from William Styron in the memoir 'Darkness Visible'. Styron observes the absence of faith in deliverance, the surety that no remedy will appear and the brevity of any form of relief. He notes that it is hopelessness, not pain, that crushes the sufferer's soul and that he or she must carry their bed of nails with them wherever they go, not able to abandon it for even a minute.

When this has been your experience for months or more, all you want is an end to your suffering. Nothing else matters. Nothing. But, as Styron rightly highlights, any faith in deliverance is absent. One of the hardest truths of this cruel illness is that it robs you of the very thing that you need to survive it: hope.

After recovering from my first bout of severe depression, which lasted for approximately eight months, I used to think that if the worst happened and it did return that it wouldn't be as bad because I would know that it would pass. I would know just how beautiful life on the other side of depression is. And after having my children I thought that I would never again feel suicidal because now I had the greatest reason that I could possibly have to endure whatever life could throw at me. I was utterly unprepared for the force with which depression would strike again, and was quickly robbed of my naïve illusions. Although in hindsight there were tell-tale signs that I was sliding back into the black hole, I was adamant that I would not, could not, suffer with depression again. I was wrong. I went from a week's holiday from work having a wonderful time with my daughter to being able to think of little but how I could end the anguish that I felt within a fortnight.

When depression strikes with such brutality, all you want is an end to the pain. That is all. No matter what else you have in your life the only thing that you can feel is the pain and anguish that crushes your soul. Even with the knowledge that depression passes, even with the experience of having overcome it once before, the belief in recovery, the hope in deliverance is… absent. And this is how depression kills. Not because the person wants to end their life, but because they want an end to the unbearable suffering. But there is no end. To the sufferer, there is no end and there will be no end. Not just for them, but for the people that love them and care for them who are helpless in the face of depression's onslaught as it robs them of the person that they knew. Leaving does not feel selfish but an end to the burden, for everybody.

I didn't want to die but I didn't know how I could continue to live. Because I wasn't living. I was surviving, from minute to agonising minute I was merely surviving but to no end. The truth is that if I had been offered a pill with the promise that I would go to sleep and never wake up, I would have taken it. In a heartbeat.

Despite being consumed with thoughts of little but ending the suffering, I couldn't do it, and I can't tell you how grateful I am for that. But that wasn't how I felt then. I felt weak. Weak that I couldn't do the one thing that would end the nightmare for me and those that cared for me. Terrified of what my life would become, with no hope for recovery, and no way of escaping.

I did escape. I recovered and I am stronger for having done so. Not everybody does recover, and for those people I have nothing but deep, deep sympathy that they were never able to reach the light. I have sympathy too for those that are left behind. Blame and accusations cannot take away the pain, but maybe a greater understanding of what leads a person to that terrible place can go some way to helping their loved ones to learn to live with it.

I will end with another observation from William Styron. He describes the pain of severe depression as unimaginable to those that have not suffered it and draws attention to the fact that it is the inability to further bear its anguish that ultimately kills in many instances. An understanding of this, and of the nature of this pain is, he suggests, vitally needed if suicides are to be prevented.

I hope that my words may contribute to this awareness.

ILLUMINATING THE SHADOW WITHIN

A shadow inside, dormant
But alive
Wish it would leave
But within me he hides

Waiting to catch me
Blind, complacent
To wreak his havoc
For his chance, ever patient

Hoping that one day
I will forget
That within he resides
A faultline in my head

To possess me wholly, consume me
Disempower
My soul, my light, my hope
He'll devour

My spirit his lifeblood
He feeds on his host
A parasitic presence
This unholy ghost

From the bowels of hell he rises
Fire feeding his flame
A burning white inferno within
This charred carcass of shame

Broken, empty
Hostile takeover complete
Talons sinking deeper
Dismantling piece by piece

Leaving but a hollow shell
Of the man I used to be
No identity but the shadow
That's disguised itself as me

And so I choose to open myself
Expose the shadow to light
To shine upon his hiding place
And keep him in my sights

My pen is thus my weapon
Emancipating words that glow
With the light of awareness to irradiate
This cancer of the soul

And may my pages wrap in comfort
Those with shadows of their own
Illuminate and brighten
Their darkened paths with hope

CLIMBING BACK FROM THE BRINK

June 2006. I'll never forget the feeling: lying in bed, limbs restless, shaking, cold sweats, heart pounding. Utterly terrified, unable to comprehend what was happening to me, a feeling of absolute dread gripping my entire being at the thought of the day ahead and the expectation on me to tutor a workshop. A workshop that I had delivered many times and had always enjoyed. I had been struggling for months and if I was to use one word to summarise what depression felt like to me it would be terror.

It's hard to accurately pinpoint a precise cause of my first severe depression but there is little doubt of the catalyst that precipitated it: on New Year's Day my then wife suffered a miscarriage. He would have been our first child. On December 4th 2005 we were married, on Boxing Day we discovered she was pregnant, on January 1st we lost our baby. At the time I felt strangely numb, empty, and in the months that followed the feeling never really left me. Over the coming months I slid inexorably into darkness.

At the onset of my first depression I had no idea what was happening to me, nor for how long I would have to endure that state of being – or more accurately, non-being. I had no idea how much further I had to fall. Surely, please surely, the bottom couldn't be much further away? I had a recurring image in my mind and sensation in my body of a boulder rolling down a cliff, gathering momentum, impossible to stop. And when I was to hit bottom – of which I had no doubt – I had no idea where I would be, nor how, or indeed if, I would be able to climb back.

Thankfully in December 2006, after five months off work, I was able to climb back from this deepest pit of despair. For good. Or so I hoped and believed, but life had other ideas. In 2013 following a prolonged period of struggle at work, the darkness engulfed me again, this time for four months during which, again, I was unable to work.

How did I escape from its seemingly unrelenting clutches? Just as it is almost impossible to attribute depression to one single thing, so too it is impossible to attribute my recovery to one particular moment or treatment. Instead, there were a combination of factors that put me on the road to recovery.

Medication

When first prescribed anti-depressants, I was scared to take them. Would they change me? Would I become dependent? If they did help me would the recovered version still be me? Would I experience the same range of emotions? I decided not to take them, thinking 'I'll beat this myself'. But I had no idea how to.

I continued to get worse until what was probably the worst day of my life. Every day with depression can feel like the worst day of your life but the events of this particular day set it apart – a complete breakdown at a work conference at Alton Towers. Not good. And so to a key moment in recovery – although recovery was still over four months away – a good friend that I'd found out had recently overcome depression himself came to see me. He was the only other person that I knew had gone through what I was experiencing. His advice – take the tablets. 'They will help, take the tablets.'

So I did, and, after my second breakdown, I continue to take them. Do they make me a different person? Well, they help to keep me a well person and that is all that matters. And just as a diabetic wouldn't feel pressured to stop taking insulin so as not to feel 'dependent' on medicine to make him healthy, neither do I feel a pressure to stop taking a medication that helps me.

Learning about depression

I read just about everything that I could to do with depression. Understanding the illness helps you to realise that what you are going through is not unique to you and it starts to make some sort of sense – 'yes, right now I'm pretty much fucked, but hey, I'm not the only one!'

A major problem for me at the time was that I could relate powerfully to the bad bits that I read – how depression can destroy your life, your relationships, your career – but not to the stories of recovery, nor the methods suggested. 'Ah yes, well, that might work for them but it wouldn't work for me because…' There was always a 'because'. Because that's another thing about depression, it's a liar. It isn't you. It is an illness and it can be overcome. I am proof.

Counselling

Without counselling I may not be here, writing this, trying to give hope to others. Counselling wasn't cheap at £90 per hour – my experiences under the NHS, which included being told by an NHS psychologist to 'cut the BS' when discussing my depression, made it pretty apparent that private therapy was my only option – but it saved my life. I can't put a price on that.

I had to overcome significant internal resistance to actually book my first session and there were two major reasons for this:

1. I was convinced nothing would help me, that I would never feel anything other than the hell that I was in, but as long as the psychologist was out there, there was some hope that there was something, someone, that could help me. However once I was to make that appointment, once I was to start the treatment that would inevitably fail because I couldn't be cured… well, what then? My life would be over. I couldn't make the call.

2. I was never going to get better and I would never be able to work again. I would lose my home and my family, in addition to my already lost mind. I would need as much money as I could to keep me from the streets for as long as possible, so I couldn't

spend any money, especially on therapy which would be an expensive waste (see number 1 above).

To my depressed mind this train of thought was more than logical, it was cast iron, self-evident truth (my psychologist taught me that I was 'catastrophising'; I can see what he meant).

Throughout recovery there was no magic bullet, no startling revelation, no moment of clarity, no one time or event that I can say, that made the difference. It was a process – one that continues to this day – of gradually understanding myself better and recognising damaging patterns of thought. Improvements seemed imperceptible but with hindsight I can see steps along the way that pointed towards recovery. There is a lesson here: to persevere when things feel hopeless; to trust the longer-term process of recovery when the hoped for 'breakthrough' doesn't appear, and to measure progress via the small things – the spontaneous smiles that begin to reappear, a peaceful, uninterrupted night's sleep.

What I did know was when the corner had been turned, when I had emerged from the blackest of nights into a brand new day, a new beginning. In 2006 it was following a holiday with my then wife to stay with my auntie in Texas. During the holiday it would be our first anniversary: a day that should have been one of happiness now bookmarking the worst year of my life and the worst of the then eleven years we had spent together. In my mind my life was over, yet I was able to determine that I would act as 'normal' as I could for the duration of the holiday, for my wife. At the very least I wanted her to enjoy her holiday after all that this illness had put her through. During the holiday 'I' started to re-emerge, living for each day only, without thinking of what would happen when the holiday was over. And when it was over I bought a PlayStation Portable and a new piano: somewhere inside I knew that I had made it, I had survived, and making two expensive purchases was a symbolic act – I no longer needed to save the money for when I was homeless.

Did I have any doubts that I had recovered? Of course, but a new voice had emerged inside that was able to shout down the voice that would seek to lock me back into the cage from which I was now free. 'Yes, I am better.'

In 2013 I had to return to work out of financial necessity despite still being ill. The evening before I was due to go back, I was ironing, and as the thought of going back to work came to mind I watched as the hairs on my arms raised and cold sweat broke the skin and began to pour around them. My return was part-time and after the first week I was exhausted; by the Friday evening, on a train home from Liverpool, I felt as though I was finished. For the entire two and a half hour journey I stared blankly out of the window; I knew that I just couldn't do it anymore, I couldn't go back to work. We would lose our home and I would lose everything.

The following day I was in the car with my wife and two children, I knew the game was up. But from somewhere came a spark of knowing – I had this weekend to enjoy my children, this was all that was left of my life. I turned and said something daft to them, and I gave the most convincing smile I could manage. I kept it up and I enjoyed that weekend with them, even when we decided to shave my hair off. On my next day at work I drove to Blackburn – I enjoyed my meeting and, driving home in glorious sunshine, I looked with wonder at the beautiful scenery that surrounded me. I knew I was better.

Recovery comes a day at a time, a step at a time. It may not be today, it may not be tomorrow, but beauty and joy in life are to be found again. A day at a time. A step at a time. With that I was able to live my life again, to enjoy my life again. To be 'me' again.

Welcome back Matthew, I missed you.

THE CAVE

Chained in the cave I stare vacantly at the wall. Shadows dance in front of me, close around me, descend across the lenses of my eyes. The shadows are my reality, monochrome filters to my claustrophobic world. I am imprisoned. Heavy weights hold me in place, anchoring me, detaining me within the cave's dark underbelly. Leaden limbs resist any impulse to struggle; futility gnaws at my soul and courses through my veins, flooding my body, numbing my senses.

The cave holds other prisoners captive, each chained, each hostage to the privations of the hostile environment. But each of us is alone. Bone-achingly alone. Each aware of the presence of others, each unable to forge a connection as words are lost in the murky cloud of chaos and confusion that our minds have become within the cave's confines. Some prisoners have been detained since childhood, knowing of no reality beyond the cave. Others entered the cave later in life. But once detained all prisoners know – all prisoners feel, deep in their marrow – that there is no reality beyond the cave. Life beyond the cave – past, present, future – is an illusion, a cruel trick of diseased minds.

Sounds burst through the shadows and echo through the cave. Sledgehammers pound rock; rock tumbles, crashing as it descends ever further into the cave's depths. The violent sounds slam through the prisoners' torpor and we writhe in anguish as the sounds collide within our skulls. Occasionally, voices can be heard from a place beyond the cave, muffled sounds that hint at an existence beyond the cave. But the voices are swallowed by the cave's dense void of darkness.

The cave chills the souls of all that enter, freezing emotions, shivering limbs. And yet, a fire roars. A blaze that lights a corner of the cave, a heat that causes skin to sweat; but the limbs resist thaw.

Day after interminable day strips the prisoner of self. The longer that I spend in the cave the more my self diminishes. Without the self there is nothing with which to relate, no reference point by which to define a place in this unknowable world. I am a shell of a being.

But I shall endure. My tortured soul shall stir. And finally, the day shall come.

Deliverance.

Light rushes into my eyes, blazing through the blinds of my mind; a dazzling luminescence that sears through the shadows that engulfed me. I walk through the light and into a new lightness of being. I view the long forgotten lands that stretch out ahead of me with wonder – for how had I never known their beauty? As I stride purposefully in the direction of new dreams, freed from the shackles of the cave, my eyes settle on the distant horizon and the promise of sunset. And as I contemplate the expanse ahead of me I realise that there are no limits to where I can go.

As long as I keep on going, I can catch the sun.

MATTHEW WILLIAMS: STIGMA FIGHTER

I was thirty one when I was first diagnosed with mental illness. I never ever expected it to happen to me (does anybody?) and it certainly wasn't a label that I wanted.

I had known that something was seriously wrong. Happiness, even for a moment, was becoming harder and harder to come by until it vanished altogether. I didn't know where it had gone nor where, or if, I could ever find it again. And as more and more days became trials to be endured, as night after night became a waking nightmare of imagined fears, I realised that it wasn't going away anytime soon and I wasn't going to overcome it alone.

And yet... and yet... it was difficult to take the steps that I needed to take to get help. After being diagnosed with depression I continued to work despite being advised by a number of people around me that I needed to take some time off. My confidence was shot to pieces and my ability to do my job was waning. Yet I felt that I had to battle through it, that taking time off would be admitting defeat. And I was afraid of being labelled: Matthew Williams, mentally ill.

I was of course aware of mental illness, but in my thirty years I had never knowingly encountered it. I wasn't a judgmental person and didn't carry negative perceptions of people that suffered mental ill-health but I was very aware of the social stigma that existed. And I was afraid. Not only of the label but of what it would mean to my future, presuming that I was to have one. How would it affect my career? Who would employ me now that I was labelled as mentally ill? Who would trust me in a pressurised role?

It's natural to be concerned about what others think of us but this shouldn't have to come at the cost of not doing what we need to do to take care of ourselves. It strikes me that I wouldn't have had these concerns had I been suffering with physical ill-health – all that would matter would be getting better and I wouldn't doubt that my friends and family would do all that they could to help me to get back to full health. I'm not looking to compare the nature and severity of physical and mental illness here, nor suggest that one is more serious than the other, but it cannot be doubted that relative social perceptions of physical and mental health differ greatly, as do the resources allocated to tackle each of them.

The associated stigma that exists around mental health was very much in my mind when struggling to persist at work in direct opposition to my declining mental health. Routine tasks became terror-filled ordeals, each charged with the potential to cruelly confirm me as a failure, as a fraud to be exposed. I continued to struggle day after day after day, until I experienced a very painful, very public breakdown at work. Not my finest hour.

The most difficult thing about my depression was how it changed me so completely, so totally, into someone, no, something, that was utterly alien to the me that I'd always presumed to be. One memory from this time remains vivid in my memory: a member of the local crisis team visited me at home and as he talked he asked me to tell him who I was. I couldn't answer. Who was I? Or rather, what was this thing, this shell that inhabited the space where Matthew used to be? Unable to answer, I turned to a photograph of Matthew holding his newborn son, smiling. 'That's him.'

This loss of self of the sufferer makes life very difficult for their loved ones as they too are unable to recognise this stranger in their midst. No matter how loving, supportive and understanding, little that they say or do seems to provide any comfort or consolation to the sufferer, entombed as he or she is within the confines of their own private hell. Little can penetrate the abyss and the futility of effort can sap the spirit of the most devoted loved ones. As important as it is for the sufferer to never lose hope that this too shall pass, so too is it important that loved ones maintain faith that the storm will subside. For when that day comes and the former sufferer has regained their capacity to feel, to love, and to participate once more in the routines of daily life, a special place will be reserved in the heart for those that were there no matter what.

The toll that depression can take on relationships with loved ones should not be underestimated and from understanding this we can perhaps glimpse an insight into the perverted mindset that can convince the sufferer that their loved ones would be better off without them. Far from a selfish act, from the sufferer's twisted perspective suicide can appear to be a longed for release and not only for themselves.

In fighting the stigma that surrounds depression a greater empathy for sufferers and a greater understanding of their particular torment can save and ultimately help to rebuild broken lives. When facing an opponent that is so determined to break the spirit, an individual's suffering is compounded by stigma that is fuelled by widely held misconceptions: questioning of the sufferer's character; assigning blame regarding how and why the affliction should strike; condemning the sufferer for a perceived willingness to allow the illness to take hold, and indeed, the commonly held misconception of whether depression is a real illness at all.

Once depression tightens its grip, the illusion of control over one's mind is exposed for the fallacy that it is. Depression is an equal opportunities affliction and it would be as well for us all to recognise this if we are to arrest its increasing incidence. According to clinical-depression.co.uk, major depression is:

'a huge problem and it is growing. Major depression is the number one psychological disorder in the western world. It is growing in all age groups, in

virtually every community, and the growth is seen most in the young, especially teens. At the rate of increase, it will be the second most disabling condition in the world by 2020, behind heart disease.'

If we are to arrest the rise of depression, it would do us well to recognise that just as none of us are immune to a heart-attack, nor are any of us beyond the reach of depression. Just as the heart is an organ, so too is the brain; just as the heart can succumb to disease if we do not keep it healthy, so too can depression strike should we be complacent of the need to cultivate a healthy mind. Far from being in control of our minds, perhaps it is instructive for us to consider psychologist Jonathan Haidt's metaphor of the elephant and rider. Haidt suggests that our emotional side can be thought of as an elephant, with our rational side as the rider. Although the rider holds the reins, it is illusory to consider him the leader as his control is limited by his relative smallness. Basically, if the elephant disagrees with the rider on which way to go there is only going to be one winner.

This is why I speak out. This is why I refuse to be silenced by stigma. I know what happens when the elephant takes charge; I've seen and felt the devastation that can be left in its wake. But I've managed to re-take the reins and brought the elephant back into harmony with its rider. And by sharing our stories, by fighting against stigma, we can help others to do the same.

FOR WHOM THE BELL TOLLS: BATTLING AN INVISIBLE ADVERSARY

Another round. My last.

I raise myself wearily from my stool. Fists tattoo my battered face, cuts and bruises telling the tale that my swollen lips can no longer form. Blows to the body fold my crumpling frame, my remaining vestiges of strength draining away through weakened limbs. Somehow the punishment is withstood, defiance summoned from somewhere deep within, legs refusing to yield to the pull of the canvas's embrace. Pressure builds within my skull and my temples pound their rhythmical beat, each pulse marking another second endured in the vice-like grip of despair.

Weakened limbs scream their protest despite the withered mind's diminished demands: unstable legs barely able to carry their damaged host; arms, long since blunted as tools of punishment, suddenly turn tormentor in their inability to afford protection from the incoming fusillade of fists. Blood trickles from the corner of my eye, sliced by the scything fury of an unforgiving aggressor; the crimson wound a gaping souvenir of my brutal reality, leaked blood traces a vivid reminder of the life that still courses through my veins, offering the slightest hope of another round, another battle, another day.

A moment of respite as my fatigued body is enveloped in the arms of my adversary, but the brief comfort only camouflages the coming assault. My arms are pinned to my sides neutralising any offensive intent that may have remained buried within this sorry shell of self.

'You got nothin' coming, man, you got nothin' coming.'

His words burrow into my brain, seeking and finding familiar company amongst scattered seeds of self-doubt, self-loathing and emotional self-harm. A crippling blow sinks into the kidney and I gasp, the warrior's mask of indifference to pain cracked by the grimace that can no longer hide the anguish that contorts my insides. The delayed signal limps along my frayed nerve endings before flushing through my legs, causing my knees to buckle at their calling. Sinking to the mat, my lungs are squeezed into paralysis as the last of my breath is disdainfully dispatched, leaving a void that my shallow wheeze cannot fill. Numbers float across my hazy consciousness...

...4, 5, 6...

'Stay down, you son of a bitch, you're through; done.'

Taunted by my invisible adversary, a spark is kindled deep within my spirit; the will to endure, the imperative to survive. Slowly, steadily, defiantly I rise. Staring into the black eyes of defeat, my gaze holds firm. Intent. I will fight.

Until the final bell tolls, I will fight.

EMPATHY FROM THE DEVIL

'Pleased to meet you, hope you guessed my name. In case you didn't my name is Depression, and I come bearing gifts.

'Well, when I say gifts I don't want you to get the wrong idea. These gifts won't be filling any stockings. No, no, no, that would be far too easy. You'll have to earn these gifts. And look, I know I'm a liar and you shouldn't believe everything I tell you, but I'm going to level with you here so you'd best be listening – these gifts are going to be worth it.

'Now, I expect this will come as scant consolation to you as you sink like a stone to the depths of your darkest ocean (sorry, I don't mean to rub it in, let's call it tough love, shall we?). I expect you know by now that I don't come bearing a life jacket. Far too easy, my friend. I can call you friend, can't I? I don't mean to sound sarcastic but I feel we're getting close, in fact I think I've become rather attached to you.

'Anyway, like I say, no life jacket. I'm not even going to offer you a hand to pull you to the surface. It's for your own good. Really, it is. I know, I know, that's easy for me to say, and, like, nobody knows what you're going through, and all you want is for somebody, anybody, to get this demon off your back (don't worry, I don't take it personally, sticks and stones and all that). The thing is, if you want to escape from this dark ocean and claim my gifts, you're going to need to learn how to swim. Others can help you to learn, but they can't swim for you. This may sound harsh given your predicament but it won't do you any favours to not hear the truth. Anyway, you must know by now that the best things in life don't come easy and you can't truly savour victory without first having tasted defeat. (Okay, so Floyd Mayweather may argue with that one but if you listened to him you'd think that money was the path to fulfilment; you're best listening to me on this one, I'm personally acquainted with many a lottery winner and know of what I speak).

'It's down to you. And I know exactly what you're going to say to me now – come on, let's hear it… There we go, 'I can't'. I. Can't. If I had a pound for every time I'd heard that… well, I'd be well retired by now, but where's the fun in that? We all need to have a purpose in life, don't we?

'See, I'm not all bad – I'm giving you a sneaky peak at one of the gifts that awaits. Purpose. If you could just consider that maybe, just maybe I'm giving you the opportunity to really find your purpose in life. Plenty of people drift through life, one day blending seamlessly into the next. But I'm showing you life from a very different perspective, and I know from experience that the view from this place can have a profound effect on those that have seen it.

'Let me give you a quote from Friedrich Nietzsche on the power of purpose,

'He who has a why to live can bear almost any how.'

'And what about Victor Frankl? Ever heard of him? He was a prisoner in Auschwitz and I'll tell you what he noticed: that in Nazi concentration camps those that were most likely to survive were the prisoners that knew they had a task waiting for them to fulfil and thus had a meaning that allowed them to transform their tragedy into triumph.

'Powerful stuff I think you'll agree. And that's not all, here's another gift that I'm offering you: empathy. Or being able to understand or share the feelings of another. You see, when you've suffered as you're suffering, it gives you an insight into the human condition that you never had before. When you witness pain and suffering in others, you can identify with it in a new and deeper way. And you are less likely to be judgemental of others that might be struggling to cope with life, like those that use drugs to block their pain or those that find themselves homeless and beg others for money.

'You'll realise that 'there but for the grace of God go I' – if you want to consider it from a religious standpoint. If that's not your thing then we can borrow from Elvis Presley: you're less likely to judge others until you have walked a mile in their shoes.

'Empathy. What's the point of that you may ask; feeling others' suffering – aren't I depressed enough already? Well, empathy leads to another gift that I can offer you – the gift of helping others.

'I know this sounds a bit soppy for me but I meant what I said, I'm not doing this for me, this is for your benefit. And, just to prove that I'm not making this up, here's what Mother Teresa had to say on the matter,

'One must really have suffered oneself to help others.'

'See? I know I'm making your life a bit shit at the moment. Okay, I'll dispense with the false modesty, I'm dragging you to the very darkest recesses of your own personal hell – well, you don't do what I've done for so long without getting to be bloody good at it. But if – or rather, when – you do swim to the surface, you'll be able to teach others to swim too. Or at the very least show them that it is possible to swim, even when you're in deep, deep water. And there are plenty of people out there that would really benefit from that. You might not even realise just how many people know me, how many you could help – you know all too well how hard it is to talk to anyone about what you're going through – but believe me, I keep myself very busy. And like I said, I'm bloody good at what I do even if I do say so myself (well, Muhammad Ali said it isn't bragging if you can back it up, and everyone loved him!).

'I'll tell you what, I can see you're having trouble believing me so let me tell you about a recent acquaintance whose story may give you a bit of hope. This guy's name was Matthew and we spent quite a bit of time together. Quality time, you might say. A fucking mess he was (pardon the language and all that but really, you should have seen him). I really did some work on him, mind you, it took a bit of persistence. I put in a couple of real good shifts – well, good for me, I can't say he enjoyed it much – and I've since paid him a couple of shorter visits, just to check in on him and see whether he could still swim.

'It turns out he's really grateful for my visits, although it would be remiss of me not to point out that he didn't think much of me at the time. And I'm pleased to say – honestly – that he loves the gifts that I left for him. He's even started a blog and reckons he can write a bit; apparently quite a few people have found that reading it helps them. Let me tell you, if he can get through it and go on to be happy then you can do it too. I don't want you to ever forget that.

'A sense of greater purpose in life, empathy and the opportunity to help others – granted they're not the latest iPhone but the novelty soon wears off with one of them and anyway, you'd only need to change it every couple of years to make sure you've got the latest model. My gifts – and these are just a few of them – can last a lifetime. How's that for value?

'So you see, I'm not all bad. Am I?'

I KNOW I AM A FUCK UP, JUST THE SAME AS YOU

'Look at you, you have to make it perfect.'

This was an accusation that I regularly faced from my best friend growing up, and for a long time I really didn't get it. My abiding memory of hearing him speak these words is from a school art lesson, as I toiled to make my work look adequate next to his unfailingly brilliant splashes of colour, texture and tone. How could he say I was perfect? Well, he wasn't, was he? When he called me a perfectionist, he recognised a trait in me that took a lot of years and a catastrophic breakdown for me to recognise in myself: I wanted to be perfect. And who wouldn't?

Thing is, life isn't like that, is it? In fact, by accepting nothing less than perfection we might actually miss those beautiful imperfections, the mistakes that can unexpectedly make life that much richer (I'm not talking about misuse of apostrophes here – that is and always will be unforgivable. See, it's apostrophes, not apostrophe's. And it's it's, not its or its'. Ahem).

Do you know the song 'Creep' by Radiohead? If so, what sound has just pushed its way into your head? It's that guitar crunch, isn't it? Yep, it's a mistake, made when Jonny Greenwood came in too early. And post-it notes. The genesis of these office essentials was in the failure to create a strong adhesive, the result being an adhesive that stuck to objects but could be pulled off easily without leaving a mark. Years later a colleague of the person that created it spread the substance on little pieces of paper to mark his place in a book and the idea was born.

Like many a self-destructive trait, perfectionism can start as a form of self-protection: if we are perfect then we are above criticism, above the harsh judgement of others. But we all know who our harshest critic is, don't we? That's right, it's that bloody voice in our heads. And I'll tell you something for nothing, he or she is full of shit. Don't believe me? Next time you flay yourself for being, heaven forbid, human, ask yourself what you would say to a friend that was telling themselves the same things that your inner critic/arsehole is telling you. I'd make a fair bet you wouldn't be agreeing with them or suggesting additional defects that they failed to mention, would you?

We live in an age of artifice where image is everything, where style overwhelmingly trumps substance and where taking a photograph of yourself can make headlines (well, if you're a Kardashian anyway). In this world a great night out is a series of selfies to show the world what a great night we are having, in between prolonged bouts of staring at the screen of a mobile phone and not talking to each other (I'll stay in with a good book, thanks).

When what other people think becomes our priority we can set ourselves up for a very bumpy ride. We fear making mistakes and revealing our flaws and imperfections. We avoid taking the kind of risks that are necessary if we are to scale the greatest heights that our talents lay the foundations for. We avoid giving our all because, well, what's the point? It will never be good enough. Someone, somewhere will always find fault.

How many of you have had the thought that you are a fraud? That if people saw the real you and not a carefully crafted illusion then… Then what? You would lose your job? Your friends? Your identity? You're not alone. I expect that the majority of the greatest minds, the greatest inventors, the greatest statesmen, the greatest sportspeople have all thought the very same thing. In fact it may have acted as fuel to the fire of their desires, igniting a work ethic and will to succeed that propelled them to their greatness. But when it comes right down to it, they were fuck ups too. Just like you, just like me: fuck ups to a man, fuck ups to a woman. How do I know? Well, because they were human just like the rest of us. We're all actors, portraying the most suitable best-self as the scene determines.

Truth is that in life's play you can be both strong and weak, a good guy and a twat, intelligent and dim, witty and boring. People are a mass of contradictions that can't easily be categorised as one thing or another. When we believe a fairytale sold as truth – the perfect marriage, the perfect job, the perfect parent – we can think that something is wrong when life just won't play ball. The myth that it's possible to be happy all the time, that there is a perfection that we can attain, can lead us into dark places where anything less than happiness or perfection is a symptom of our failure. But one thing that I've learned in recent years is that whilst the fairytale may be where we'd like to live, our greatest lessons and gifts are often found within our nightmares. After enduring a dark night of the soul we can see that sometimes our greatest journeys begin from the darkest of places.

I still have that critic whispering in my ear. He's there every time I write, sitting on my shoulder as my finger is poised above the 'publish' button. 'It's trite. It's pat. It's bollocks. You're just saying what has already been said much better by others.' But I hit the button anyway because, really, all of that could be true but who cares? As I write, my uncle has just died and two friends have lost loved ones in terribly tragic circumstances. Life really is short and it can be taken from us at any moment. Best to spend as much of it as you can doing the things that matter to you, because in the end will it really matter what anybody else thought?

DIVINE MADNESS

A recent conversation with a friend prompted one of those deep and meaning(ful/less – delete as applicable) musings of mine. The conversation touched on spiritual awakenings, mental breakdowns and the difference between the two. Now, I'm conscious that not everybody holds much truck with the idea of spirituality and in many minds the idea is anathema to the scientific, hard-evidence, Dawkins era in which we live, but for me there's always been some kind of sense that there is something else, a side of me that craves connection with something deeper and greater than myself.

I think it's fair to say that this is part of the human condition, leading to a sense of searching, of questing that I expect all of us feel in one way or another during our lives. Such questing for connection, fulfilment and a need to find meaning in something greater than us is evident throughout human history, its expression finding form in the development of religions, music, ritual and art. In this particular conversation, the question of whether someone is experiencing a spiritual awakening or mental breakdown was raised and the idea intrigued me. Discussing both of these things can feel socially awkward and can leave us feeling vulnerable and judged by all those saner, more rational people out there; those that are holding their shit together and thriving in this material world of ours, while we wonder whether they think we're losing the plot, or indeed, we wonder it ourselves.

I've lost the plot before, publicly and spectacularly, some would say humiliatingly. Having a public breakdown in front of nigh on a hundred respected colleagues is a great leveller, let me tell you. Thing is, I didn't feel judged – at the time I was utterly incapable of feeling anything other than total mental anguish and a desire for it to end, with no regard for how that end should come about. Blunt, bleak – that's the reality of mental illness. Neither too did I feel judged when I'd recovered and had to face my colleagues again; I'd had some very kind messages of support and in place of any shame or embarrassment I felt a sense of strength and self-assurance that only clawing my way back from the jaws of hell could uncover. And if that sounds overly dramatic, trust me, there is no need for embellishment.

Having lost the plot I am less concerned these days about what people think about me, and when you've had to give every ounce of yourself just to be able to live again it can liberate you from the more trifling concerns about what anybody else thinks about how you should live your life. I expect that when I first began to write and my posts started to appear on friends' timelines some will have thought I was losing the plot again. Maybe in some ways I was, I certainly wasn't in a good place at the time (and that isn't a reference to Tamworth). What did I think? I thought that something was happening to me, that that time of suffering in my life was important; that what was happening to me was significant. Actually no, I didn't think that. I knew it. Deep in my bones I knew it, and wherever it was to take me and whatever people were to think was not my business – my business was to write and to get out of myself whatever it was that needed to find its expression.

So here I am today and people will think what they want to think, that's not my business; my business is to follow my path in life, to live honestly and true to myself so that I become the best version of me that I can, and in doing so life will offer opportunities for me to thrive, for the best of me to be put to purposeful use to make a difference beyond any self-interest. How do I know that life will offer such opportunities? Faith. Faith in life, faith that there is a greater purpose to my life, and faith that I will find whatever answers I need to find along the way within me. Faith that somehow, to someone, I will make a difference.

Is this some kind of spiritual awakening? Is there even such a thing? Perhaps, perhaps not. I think of former heavyweight champion George Foreman, a mean and surly bully of the ring, a brute of a man that delighted in the destruction he wreaked on the powerful, reducing formidable and feared fighters to rubble in the ring. The same George Foreman that 'died' in his dressing room following defeat in 1977 and was born again, utterly convinced from that instant to this that he had been anointed by Jesus and that his life had a new meaning that he had to find. The same George Foreman that gave up boxing and its associated fame and fortune to preach on street corners and establish his own church and a community centre for local youths. The same George Foreman that returned to the ring ten years later reformed, the same devastating punch and immense strength now accompanied by a jocular smile, words to inspire and a deeper purpose – to spread the word of the God that he gave his life to and to raise money to keep his community centre for local youths from closing.

Was his experience real? Did God talk to him in that dressing room in 1977? At the time, those around him questioned his sanity; did he experience a breakdown?

What is real? Does it matter?

Mental breakdown? Spiritual awakening? Maybe they are different sides of the same coin. I don't know what this last few years has been about for me but what I do know is this – I have learned to listen more and more to my instincts and more and more I see how accurate they are, how the sense about something unknown turns out to be the truth when I am really prepared to listen.

Is there a greater purpose unfolding for me? In a rational age what are the chances of that being the case? Well, I expect the odds to be very long indeed, but then the very fact that you and I are even here at all is based on biological odds of hundreds of millions to one. Whatever the 'literal' answer to the question of purpose I will find meaning, and maybe that's the point. In Foreman's case, regardless of what anybody else thought he took his reality and utterly transformed his life and the lives of many others. He achieved greater success in his second career than anybody ever imagined, driven by a purpose beyond himself.

That is real. That is beyond any dispute. And maybe that is what really matters most.

IF I COULD TURN BACK TIME

I write this at the time of Britain's historic EU referendum. The people of Britain have spoken; it's time to leave.

As the country prepares to take one giant leap into the unknown, it would seem that some are no longer as certain of their position as they were a few days ago. Ordinary voters and politicians alike now face the reality of the challenges that our new dawn is sure to bring, and as that reality raises new questions, we hear that some voters are declaring that they would vote differently should the option be given today, we see politicians back-tracking from the promises of what a vote for leave would mean.

This is to be expected; when facing an unknown future the desire to retreat back to what is safe and known can be strong, even if the safe and known present isn't a happy one. But however hard a decision is to make, in reality that is the easy bit. It is how we act on our decisions that determine the consequences that will define us, and it is through our actions that we speak; not through our words, not through our decisions, but through our consequent actions.

Be careful what you wish for – sometimes it is when we get what we want that the real work starts, the work needed to make the new future a better home than the present. Building a better home can be a difficult, time consuming, painful process; one that requires us to maintain the hope and conviction that was used to lay the new foundations if we are to weather the storms that will inevitably lash against us as we build.

Leaps into the great unknown don't always begin with our choices. New beginnings can be thrust upon us against our will, resisted with every fibre of our being, fought against with the futility of Canute trying to hold back the tide. And once the waves have washed over us and swept us away, we have no choice but to stay afloat by whatever means we can, until the waters calm and we are able to swim towards a new shore not of our choosing. Battling harsh elements, whether through choice or circumstance, can lead us to ask ourselves whether it will all be worth it. Our words seasoned with the bitter tang of regret as we ask ourselves, 'could I, should I, would I have done things differently, if only I'd have known where I would be today?'

Political events of recent days have prompted this reflection in my own life: for all the blessings for which I'm grateful I can't honestly look in the mirror and say that I am happy with where I find myself at this point in my life. And there are two significant, linked events that steered me onto my present course, neither of which was of my choosing: depression and divorce. If I could rewind the film and re-direct my life's story, would depression and divorce still feature?

Depression? Unhesitatingly, unquestioningly, yes. Remain. Don't get me wrong, I wouldn't wish depression on a single human being and I hope more than anything that I never have to feel its soul-crushing presence again for as long as I may live. But having escaped from its clutches I wouldn't remove it from my backstory. The chapters that it wrote in my life taught me more than perhaps any other. They added depth to my character and broadened my understanding of what it is to suffer, what it is to be human, and what is takes to face your demons and emerge resolute. In the cost:benefit analysis, depression has given me far more than it has taken.

Divorce? Well, that's harder to answer.

Where the passage of time has revealed the gifts of depression, divorce's gifts remain hidden. Almost two years on from separation the reverberations are still acutely felt. Not just from the divorce itself but from subsequent events. Doubts, insecurities, heartaches and worries, fears and tears – all remain fresh, all still feature to a greater or lesser extent. Amongst this unappealing cocktail of thoughts, feelings and emotions, it is hard to see the cherry on top.

I maintain my hope and belief that it will be found. I hold onto my faith that a greater good will come from this, although the strength of my grip varies from day to day. Following divorce I have had some wonderful times and met some wonderful people that I am grateful came into my life. When considering the question of regrets in my life I've always had little time for them, being of the view that I always did the best I could with the tools available to me at the time, and that whatever mistakes I made led me to where I am today. But would I choose to be where I am today? Honestly? No.

That being said, in asking whether I would remove divorce from the story of my life, I would still have to say no. Because I have to move forwards, I have to stride purposefully into my future and that won't happen with one foot stuck in the past, lodged between regret and self-pity. The transition from husband and father to divorcee and single father is a difficult one, and truth be told my life still feels as though it is in transition. I'm making the most of it as best I can, trying to live as fully and contentedly in the moment as I can, but a better future is never far from my hopes.

I look forward to the as yet unwritten chapters that I desire to be better than those that have come before, that will reveal the hidden meanings, the pregnant possibilities that currently remain buried in those past chapters of heartbreak. But those better chapters won't write themselves. And whether as the creator of circumstance or in reaction to it, it is how I act and what I do that will determine whether those chapters will be happy, will be meaningful, and will add substance to my story.

Regrets? I've had a few, but then again, none of that matters now. All that matters is the next step, for that is the only one available. And I hope to learn the lessons of the past so that my step is assured, and heading in the right direction.

HOW COOL IS MENTAL ILLNESS?

For those of us that have suffered mental ill health we are fortunate to live in an age of growing awareness, viral social media campaigns and positive stories of individuals with mental illness; in past generations we would have faced ridicule, institutionalisation or worse. In fact, as more and more people speak out about their struggles – from Coronation Street's Bev Callard to boxer Frank Bruno, from comedian Ruby Wax to model Cara Delevingne – nowadays if you've suffered with mental illness it's possible to feel part of quite an exclusive club.

Never mind Vinnie Jones's Wimbledon of the 1980s, this is the Crazy Gang to be in, and it's us that's taking on the world and winning. Hardly a day goes by where we don't hear a story of somebody opening up candidly about their 'year from hell', or publicising their new book in the best-selling 'misery memoir' genre with the attendant series of newspaper serialisation exclusives.

It's not difficult to understand why – stories of overcoming the odds, of facing life's demons and defeating them, of victories in the most trying of circumstances, of great achievement born of great suffering – these stories are as old as time and speak to the inner struggles, both large and small, that we all face on our journeys through life. And in the UK in particular, we love it when the underdog triumphs.

Now, I don't know about you, but if I never hear the word 'Brexit' ever again it will be too soon. If I never see Nigel Farage on my television screen ever again it will be too soon. If I never read another Daily Mail headline about AIDS-ridden EU migrant rapists claiming all of our benefits ever again, it will be too soon (or did I just imagine that one?). Because no matter how important the subject, no matter what is at stake, there's only so much of it we can take. In our fast-paced, 24 hour, news/opinion/speculation based, social media world, sometimes we get tired of being told what to think and do and we just want the noise to stop.

'Mental illness kills every day.'
'That's terrible. Could I order a skinny latte, please?'

Interest and concern can give way to apathy as we face the ever growing demands made of us in our own lives whilst all around us white noise hisses the struggles of others. If we feel we are being force-fed mental illness stories often enough, apathy can turn to cynicism, with questions about whether the appeal of being in this popular and cool new mental illness club is actually a PR ploy to create interest in a new film, album or book; or, away from the shimmering glare of celebrity, whether it gives substance and depth to otherwise inconsequential lives.

When I started writing, it wasn't with the intent of writing about mental health; no, I intended to bore everybody with woe-is-me stories of divorce and heartbreak, dating and giving up on dating. But it very quickly became apparent to me that I needed to write about it. If my writing was to be honest then I couldn't not talk about it as it has had such a significant impact upon my life, how I view my life now and how I try to deal with the challenges I face. And yes, I am conscious of adding to what some may perceive to be noise around mental health, of ramming it down people's throats, of pushing it in front of their faces via another new post update on Facebook.

'Bloody hell, Matty's bangin' on about his depression again. He'll be writing a bloody book about it before long, I tell you...'

But here's why I do it – this club has more than enough people in it already. If I can stop anybody from joining it, if I can help just one person to escape from it, then what I say is worthwhile. If one person can take these words and hang onto them, can use them to light their way and help them to escape their cave, then it really doesn't matter what anybody else thinks.

In reality the mental illness club really isn't very exclusive – anybody can come in. Your friends, your colleagues, even your children – it doesn't turn away under eighteens – any one of them could find themselves gaining membership. Some of them may not be able to leave. I don't want that, so I will keep talking. And if you are still listening, thank you.

THE THINKER

I was always a thinker. Scratch that, I was always an overthinker. It's not a choice, it's just the way my brain works. Most of the time it's a good thing: a proclivity to think and a questioning nature helps me – I hope – to view things from a wider point of view than I may have done otherwise; to recognise the limits of my own life experience and the filters through which I make sense of the world and my place in it, leading to a desire to want to know more, to learn, to better myself. To know myself.

But sometimes, my brain stops working. Thinking becomes stilted, thoughts are lost in a confusing tangle forming knots of negativity and fear, strangling expression as words disintegrate in the mind's fog and the connection between brain and mouth is scattered with obstacles, around which sentences break and struggle to reform. At its worst, during severe depression, my ability to think clearly and to express myself was lost almost completely; dead eyes a giveaway to the lack of spark inside, the brain a black whirlpool of rumination swallowing all thoughts and subsuming them beneath the only truths that it would recognise,

'You're not good enough,' 'you're going to lose everything,'
'you'll never get better.'

Faced with a self that was totally alien to the idea of self that had propelled me through over thirty years of a largely charmed life, I was forced to confront who I thought I was; to question what

I thought, how I thought, and why I thought in the way that I did. Pulling apart the threads was hard, so fucking hard; sometimes it's only when forced to confront ourselves that we can appreciate just how lucky we are, to be able to travel through life safe in our assumptions of who we are, comfortable in the skin – and the mind – that we inhabit.

When I look back on this time I see something else too: I see the power of not thinking. Just as the athlete that trains his body to the limit needs time for relaxation and recovery to allow damaged muscles to repair and strengthen, so too does the mind need to switch off to allow the crashing waves of thoughts to subside and settle into calmer waters. This is easier said than done amidst the raging mind-storms of severe depression, but as I reflect on the moments of calm amidst my storms – getting lost in a game on the PS3, sinking into a good book, a pub quiz, a game of darts – I see my mind being tended to every bit as much as it was during psychotherapy.

Amongst the fog there was something that did become very clear to me during this period. A thought that articulated itself with clarity and with conviction, a core belief that I was left with when everything else was stripped away. At this point, without wishing to sound melodramatic, I didn't want to live anymore. Not because I wanted to die but because I couldn't face the crumpled and torn facsimile of life that stretched ahead of me, one in which I was totally alone, with no recognisable identity and with no hope of breaking free of the mental anguish that was my constant, unrelenting burden. It was from this state of non-being that a core-belief crystallised: life presents each of us with defining challenges and it is our job to learn the lessons that are held within them. Whatever reason there was for the state in which I found myself in, I was convinced that there was a reason, that it was my task to find this reason and that there was no way of escaping this task; whether in this life or the next, I had to find it. I had no choice but to live through it and to learn.

The fact that I sit here writing this is testament to the fact that I did. I learnt a lot, and from that dark, lonely morass came a better understanding of self; of my hopes, my fears, and of the inner resources I possess with which to face life's inevitable future trials (and they have certainly been put to the test since). The deep, stagnant pit of depression is the darkest, loneliest place I've ever been to and my deepest hope is that I will never find myself there again. To be honest, it's a thought that I can hardly bear. I try to maintain a vigilant awareness of my moods and thoughts but have found that this can come at its own cost; when vigilance over-reaches and begins to question what would otherwise have been considered the normal ebb and flow of moods, where features of personality can be translated as character flaws, faultlines which lead to the darkest parts of myself, parts that however deeply buried, however long they lay dormant, I mustn't forget are there.

I think about it, I write about it, and I've learned. I continue to learn, and to accept that within me lay both the seeds of my collapse and the tools of recovery. I try to keep my tools sharp and more than ever I try to accept myself just as I am and to allow myself to feel whatever mood I'm feeling, without judgement and without resistance. I remind myself that it will pass and that I don't always have to know the answers, there doesn't always have to be a reason.

Maybe it's just me; and maybe I'm okay just as I am.

WITH A LOT OF HELP FROM MY FRIENDS

Time to Change, the national organisation committed to increasing awareness of mental health and reducing stigma and discrimination, launched a new campaign in February 2017 aimed at men encouraging them to talk about mental health and to support their mates if they think they might be struggling. I've been privileged to be involved in this campaign and to have my story featured in the campaign's launch. But it isn't just my story, it's also the story of my two oldest friends, Craig and Simon, and how they were both there for me when I most needed them, helping in each of their own unique ways.

This chapter is based on something I wrote that was featured in the campaign. If my writing has one overarching theme it is of overcoming life's challenges. Not only can we come through difficult times, we can positively thrive following adversity, living richer, more fulfilling lives not in spite of but because of the very circumstances that at one point were dragging us under. My involvement in this campaign is testament to this fact, representing a journey from believing that my life was over and that I had nothing to offer life, to playing a role in a major campaign that will help many hundreds of thousands of people that find themselves in similar circumstances. However dark things may seem at times in our lives, we never know what the future has in store for us; amazing things could be just around the corner and we should always hold onto that.

♥

It's all about people, isn't it? Life, that is. As we look back on our happiest memories, for the most part it's the people that shared those moments with us that made them so special; it's people that add the colour and character to life's precious moments. It's people that can make the biggest difference to us when life reveals its darker side, when we grieve and when we hurt. And it's the people that share with us our tears as well as our laughter that we hold dearest to us.

I've seen life's darker side. Having suffered with crippling bouts of depression in both 2006 and 2013, I've wondered whether the darkness would ever lift, whether moments of laughter would ever visit my door again, whether the 'me' that I once knew would ever find his way back. The 'me' that I had been was gone, replaced by a broken shell of what once was, a mass of pain and despair; of fear, terrible fear of what would become of me and who would still be there at the end of it, if indeed an end would come.

But they were there. My oldest friends were there for me throughout, and I'll never, ever forget that and I can never thank them enough.

Craig, my oldest friend who I met at nursery and who has been there to listen ever since, to pick me up when I've been let down and disappointed, when I've been dumped, when I've been angry, when I've been dumped, when I've been hurt, when I've been dumped (you get the picture). He was there for me as my Best Man on my wedding day; he was also there when I wondered how I could face another day, when getting out of bed was the limit of my achievements, when the chatty, fun Matthew was replaced by one for whom smiling was an impossibility. He was there, every week to take me out and just be there, reminding me of who I really was beneath the illness and letting me know that somebody believed in me, and that however bad things were I could count on him being in my corner.

Simon, my friend since I asked him whether he was a boy or a girl on our first day of primary school. A man so popular it's only a matter of time before he has a lounge named after him in his local (or a poker table at least); a friend that at times over the years I've lost touch with as our lives took us in different directions and to different places, but who I am always able to pick up with as if we'd never been away. The friend that took me out to play darts every week during my second illness even though his dad was terminally ill. At a time when others less understanding could have – and maybe would have – thought, 'What have YOU got to be depressed about?', he was there, giving me brief respite from my waking nightmare whilst reminding me that 'trebles are for show but doubles are for dough.'

It's hard to overstate just how much their support meant to me. One thing that mental illness teaches you (or taught me at least) is just how much inner strength and resource you have, but in the midst of it nothing could seem further from the truth. Between them, my friends reminded me that my illness wasn't me, that I had a lot to offer and would one day be me again, and that just for an hour or two I could escape from my broken mind and focus on the 'now' of a pub quiz or throwing a dart. Whilst being able to recognise this at the time, it is only from the promised land of recovery that I can truly appreciate just how much of a difference their support made to me, how much it helped me in a recovery that at the time didn't seem possible.

There is so much stigma and misunderstanding that surrounds mental illness and this is acutely felt when you are surrounded by its fog. For men in particular it can be difficult to admit to, when 'being a man' is associated with being strong and tough and not admitting to needing help from anybody, from putting a shelf up to admitting that your life is falling apart around you and that you're scared and you can't cope. Sometimes we can't admit this to ourselves, but what we can all do is look out for our friends and be there for them when they are struggling, to notice when they're not quite themselves and could use a mate in their corner. We don't need to understand mental illness to do this, we just need to understand that our friend needs to know we're there for them, whether to talk, to listen, to tell bad jokes or to give them an affectionate punch on the arm.

Some people claim not to believe in mental illness; well, millions of people do believe in Santa Claus and the Tooth Fairy but their belief doesn't make them real. Similarly, not believing in mental illness doesn't make it not real, it IS real, and it can strike anybody at any time. Believe me, if it happens to you then you will KNOW that it is real, and you will be left in no doubt that you are very ill and that you can't get through it alone. Nobody chooses mental illness, and from experience I can honestly say I wouldn't wish it on anybody. But like most difficulties in life it teaches us things too, and one of the biggest lessons you learn is who is there for you when you most need them to be.

We can all be that friend. Be in your mate's corner, you may never know just how much difference it could make.

Craig's advice for helping a friend with depression

'I really struggled to know whether I was helping or not during his really dark times, but now I know that I did (because he's told me!). For me it was just about spending time with him, going for a coffee or a drink, letting him talk and get things off his chest. I think he knows me well enough to know that I would not judge him no matter what.'

Simon's advice for helping a friend with depression

'I'd suggest bringing up things from your own personal life that the person may not know. It doesn't have to be anything major – but being a bit more open about things, especially as a man, can often encourage a friend to do the same. You never know when that moment may come when they just need to talk to you, or share something with you. The more open you are with them, the more likely they will be to confide in you rather than keep it hidden away.'

MENTAL HEALTH
WITH LOUIE SPENCE

'Youth hostelling with Chris Eubank...'

Now, it's fair to say I've had some strange, surreal, brilliant experiences as a result of my writing but today tops the lot. It does not involve budget accommodation and Mr Christopher Livingstone Eubank Esq but it's not far off: Mental Health with Louie Spence. For ITV's Lorraine. Yep, I didn't see that one coming, especially not this week.

Truth be told I wasn't having the best of weeks when I checked my work emails to see a message from Time to Change, whose brilliant 'In Your Corner' campaign I am fortunate to be featured in. It is that campaign that led directly to this opportunity. I was invited to be part of a group conversation to be led by Louie Spence of Pineapple Dance Studios fame. Louie has himself suffered with mental health problems and the feature is part of a series highlighting men's mental health. Would I like to be involved?

After careful consideration lasting approximately 1.16 seconds I said, well, I said yes of course. I'm a firm believer in saying yes to life's weird and wonderful opportunities and the opportunity to be part of something that raises awareness of an issue that is so close to my heart was not one that I was going to refuse. Oh, and I'd get to be on the telly. (Okay, I confess, I'm not entirely selfless).

All that said, saying yes did cause pause for consideration, coming as it does at a time when I have been contemplating the fine line that can at times be walked between wanting to learn from my experiences of mental ill health and use them in advocacy to help raise awareness, and the potential danger of anchoring myself in a very traumatic time of my life that it took an awful lot to pull myself out of.

How to find the correct balance? It's something I've been thinking about and it was brought to mind on my journey to the central London location where we were to be filming. As my driver – yes, ITV sent a driver to pick me up from the train station #bigtime – fought his way through London traffic and approximately eighty seven red lights, I was reminded of how, as a frequent traveller in my job, I would rather endure a longer journey throughout which I am constantly moving forward than spend large portions of time sitting still on an ultimately quicker journey. It seems an appropriate analogy – the key question is whether what I am doing ultimately means that my life is moving forward. It's something that I shall be keeping in mind.

Filming the segment was a brilliant experience and it was fascinating and eye-opening for me to hear the experiences of the four other men involved. The whole experience really brought home to me what has been one of the greatest benefits of having experienced mental ill health – a greater ability to empathise and connect with others that have shared similar traumatic, profoundly life altering experiences. And if that sounds as though it could be a bit, well, depressing, it isn't. Quite the opposite in fact. As was highlighted during our conversation, such shared experiences really do enable you to open up to others, people that you perhaps wouldn't have thought you had anything in common with, and connect in a way that feels quite unique.

The whole experience also reminded me, once again, of one of the greatest life lessons that my encounters with depression and recovery have taught me: you really do never know just what waits around the corner for you, and the very worst moments of your life really can – and I guess often do – propel you towards some of the very best.

In that lesson there lies hope, and that is the one thing that we should never lose. I sincerely wish that through having opportunities to share my experiences I can do my little bit to bring hope to others in times of suffering and doubt. And as I sit typing this in a Tesco's Costa, adrenaline subsiding and the reality of a 5.45 am start to the day catching up with me, a further truth echoes in my mind: whether it's your best day or your worst day, remember,

'This too shall pass.'

PART 3

DATING, BLOODY HELL: DISPATCHES FROM THE ROCKY ROAD TO ROMANCE

DATING, BLOODY HELL

Dateline: 1 month post-separation

Let's lift the mood a bit here. Dating... Bloody hell, dating.

When to start dating after a marriage split? This is the first thing to ask yourself. Well, after you've got over the initial whack of separation and entertained the possibility that somewhere out in the world there may be somebody else that will be, maybe, a little bit interested in you.

A few weeks after my marriage broke down, a female friend offered me some kind words that boosted my confidence and led me to look into online dating. I did my research – be prepared and all that. But how prepared could I be? The world of dating was a whole lot different as a forty year old in 2014 than it was to a twenty one year old in 1995. Truth is I'd never dated anyway really, I'd had a girlfriend for two years from the age of eighteen and then two weeks after we split I met my future (ex) wife.

The last time I'd started a relationship, communication outside of meeting up was using the phone (and a landline phone at that) in my parents' bedroom hoping that nobody else would overhear. Not easy in a family of five. In the intervening nineteen years, the internet had opened up a whole new world, and Matty-lad was about to enter it. It was only a month after separation, which may seem indecently hasty, but I knew my marriage was over and had started to accept it, as hard as that was. And I wanted to get out there and meet new people, see what the modern world of dating was all about.

If I'm honest there was another motive too. One of the most potent poisons of the male post-separation mind is the thought of your ex meeting somebody new. At this point starts a battle between the rational, reasonably together self, and the paranoid, insecure and vulnerable self. In my case this opened two potential paths:

1. Find a new relationship
2. Find a way to get, errrrr, laid
   (without putting too fine a point on it)

The thinking behind the latter was that getting this under the belt, pardon the pun, would somehow soften the blow when the inevitable happened and my ex 'moved on'. My research, which included the internet and my brother, revealed my two options: a paid site where I could meet nice (hopefully) people that were serious about looking for a decent guy, and a 'hook up' site with people that may well be nice but would also be a little, well, let's say looser with their timetable for getting intimate. And with their undies. I'll focus for now on my experience of the hook-up site. (I expect this will not come as a disappointment to you, dear reader). I will relate two stories and where they led me.

The first involved a guy in Yorkshire who was looking for somebody to, let's say, 'look after' his wife while he watched. WTF???? People do this??? Okay, let's find out what the hell this is all about. I expressed a cautious interest in finding out more. They'd never done this before but had talked about it for a while and were looking to give it a go (at this point I will stress that his role was to purely be an observer while the magic happened). They weren't really sure how to go about it but his task was to screen potential suitors. He asked what I would do if I were to be the chosen one.

Bloody. Hell.

I let my imagination take flight and typed away. I won't recount the grisly details, let's just say that Christian Grey wasn't losing any sleep. Despite that, I received a message back saying I'd made the shortlist (note: I did not send any pictures, it wasn't THAT kind of 'short' list, no man wants to be on that list). He would be in touch soon to look at next steps. In the meantime, he kindly sent me some naked pictures of his wife. Cheers.

The second story has as its lead character a twenty one year old woman that got in touch telling me she was into 'Extreme'. Once again, I did my research and apparently she wasn't talking about the soft-rock band from the early 1990s (incidentally, their most famous song – not a long list to select from admittedly – 'More Than Words', is about trying to get his woman to give him a... well, I'll let you fill in the blanks). Anyway, my research revealed that what it actually meant was that she liked to be dominated, and she elaborated by explaining that I could go round to her house and do whatever I wanted. She wasn't talking about her ironing.

I asked myself, what the hell happens to a twenty one year old that makes her willing to do that? I've always liked to think of myself as a decent guy and realised that what I wanted was connection with somebody. And really, when it came right down to it, I'd rather spend a night in a restaurant with a nice woman sharing good food and conversation than a meaningless lay with a stranger, and a possibly damaged one at that. The account was deleted and pathway one was chosen – let's try to find a nice woman to get to know and see where the road would take us.

I don't know if Mr Sex Person found anyone to get to grips with his wife. Apparently they were a bit alarmed by some of the 'disturbing' messages that they received.

Who'd have thought it?

A STRANGE PHENOMENON

Dateline: 1 year 4 months post-separation

I read. A lot. True to type, one of the first things that I did when my ex-wife and I split up was to buy myself some books on dealing with separation and divorce. When reading about the turbulent emotions and feelings that I could expect to feel – after the numbness would wear off – something that was said struck me as curious: don't be surprised if you find the break-up of your first post-marriage relationship to be more difficult than the ending of your marriage.

At the time of reading, the thought of a future relationship seemed a distant prospect and I continued reading in the hope of finding words that could offer solace in the immediate post-marriage void that I found myself in. But that statement stuck, staying somewhere in the back of my mind. Well, what do you know – it turned out to be true.

As I came through the painful early days of separation, wishing that I was a year further down the line when life would be a new kind of normal, I was able to accept that my marriage was over. And as I adjusted to my new post-marriage life and was able to start to feel optimistic about the future, I began to feel hopeful about the prospect of dating again. And, bloody hell, did I strike lucky. A month after my marriage ended and within a few hours of becoming a fully paid-up member of the dating website Match, I found myself talking to a very beautiful, very funny woman. Within a week, and after many messages, we met and soon were in a relationship. After a nineteen year relationship, everything was new and exciting – the last time I started seeing someone there wasn't even such thing as text messaging. We were together for ten months and in that short time there were many happy moments.

Divorce turns your whole world upside down and with it there are almost constant adjustments that you have to make; finding somewhere to live (three places in less than a year), adapting to becoming a part-time parent, adapting to being a single parent, managing money, dealing with solicitors (and paying for them), balancing your responsibilities, dealing with the first post-split Christmas, first anniversary, first new relationships – on both sides. Perhaps it's not surprising that most first post-marriage relationships fail. In the midst of dealing with all of the above, can you really be the partner that another deserves?

When my new relationship ended in July 2015 – amicably due to being at different stages of our post-divorce lives – I told myself that I would be fine. After all, nothing could be worse than your marriage ending and the break-up of your family, surely? But it seems that all of the practical adjustments that you make as your marriage fails can create a sort of scab over the emotional wounds of your marriage split. In the thrill of a new relationship there is a salve for those wounds and you can forget that they are there. But when the realisation dawns that the new relationship is over, that scab is ripped away and the wounds are opened, wider than before with twice the loss to grieve.

Immediate post-marriage relationships have been called a number of things – 'rebounds', 'inbetweeners' – denoted as mere footnotes in the stories of our lives. I can't speak for anybody else, but I don't feel that way. In the overall story of my life that chapter is a short one, but it isn't a footnote. She was the right person for me at that time, she made me smile, laugh, and rediscover a sense of fun and happiness that I came to realise had been missing from my life for a long time. Our relationship will always have a special place in my heart.

When reading a much-loved book, we don't always want to turn that final page, wishing that we could spend more time with the characters that we have grown to love. I don't want our story to end. I'd take her back tomorrow but it's too late, she's with somebody else now. All good stories must end sometime.

IF YOU'VE LOST YOUR FAITH IN LOVE & MUSIC

Dateline: 1 year 5 months post-separation

Music is a huge love of mine and many of the most significant moments in my life have their own special soundtrack. This has its downside when it comes to the end of a relationship as some of our favourite songs can become tainted by the pain of association with happier times. After my latest break up, a particular song has become stuck on a loop in my mind: 'Everything Reminds Me of Her' by the late Elliott Smith.

Places that have been familiar to me throughout my life are suddenly associated exclusively with memories from a period of only ten months. It seems to be a particularly perverse trick that our minds play on us but I guess it's part of the process in helping us to accept and deal with what we have lost and move on.

Music has a significant place in my mind right now for another reason. One of my favourite bands, The Libertines, sang that should you lose faith in love and music then the end won't be far away. One of the challenges of life post-depression is in knowing when how you are feeling is a normal response to challenging times, and when it is a signifier of something bigger, something darker. It can be hard to know. Thoughts and behaviours that in hindsight can be seen to have precipitated a major depression can seem minor, insignificant and almost unnoticeable at the time. It's important to maintain a healthy balance between not being complacent about depression's ability to strike, and not interpreting the inevitable dark days as signs of an impending storm.

One of the characteristics of depressive illness is rumination, endless negative thoughts playing in a constant loop in your head. And yes, everything reminds me of her. But I have learned that one of the signs that I need to be vigilant about is losing my love of music – on both occasions that I have been ill this was an early warning sign. I haven't lost it. I enjoy singing along with my children to our favourite playlist in the car and I will still put something on to listen to as I drop off to sleep. Admittedly, there is probably a little more Damien Rice than is emotionally healthy but to quote John Lennon, whatever gets you through the night.

Divorce is devastating and its aftershocks ripple through your life and relationships for a long time. But despite my own experiences, my faith in love and music remain strong.

NEEDLE IN A HAYSTACK: DATING FOR THE DIVORCED

Dateline: 1 year 5 months post-separation

Who'd have thought dating could seem so much like, well, hard work?

Now, the obvious point to highlight from the off is that I can only speak for myself; if Brad Pitt or, errrrrrr, Harry Styles somehow found themselves on Tinder or Plenty of Fish, chances are it might not be much of a chore. But, for this forty-something from Middlesbrough, it ain't easy, I can tell you. Even for a Brian Cox lookalike.

In the first flush of single life entering the brave new world of online dating (well, new to someone that has been in a relationship for nineteen years anyway), the overriding sense was one of excitement and possibility. And, in spite of an odd detour (dating, bloody hell...) my first experience of online dating – where I met a wonderful woman very quickly – turned out to be far from representative of the reality of seeking your perfect partner online.

Cards on the table time – I'm a bit weird. Although I'm not detecting many sharp intakes of breath here, let me explain what I mean by that: I'm not really designed for casual relationships and one night stands. I know, I know, I'm a bloke but what can I say, faulty wiring, I guess. I've always been the same, I prefer to get to know somebody and want to meet somebody that I can really connect with, someone that I can laugh with as we navigate life's ups and downs together. Someone whose presence in my life makes me a better person and brings out the best that I have to offer. So you see, basically I'm soft as shite.

Anyway, so far she's not on Tinder. Or Plenty Of Fish. Or okay, Cupid… Hell, I'm getting depressed just typing those out. And really, I haven't done too badly, I suppose. I've met eight or nine women for dates. One week I had dates with three woman planned (separately I might add). To many that might sound great, but you know what? It isn't. Well, not for me anyway, because it's not about numbers, it's about meeting somebody that's right. And that's harder than I guess I thought it would be. Don't get me wrong, I've met plenty of nice people. I don't really have any dating disasters to speak of (sorry to disappoint you) and I'm glad for the experiences that I've had – in the end you learn from them and when one day in the future I am with that special person I expect I will appreciate her all the more. But when you are looking for that special someone, especially at a relatively advanced age and after nearly nine years of marriage, it can all get… dispiriting. The dating treadmill has tired me out, many times. And not in THAT way.

There are only so many times that you can get to know somebody new, only so many times you can go on a first date, only so many times you can have the same conversation with different people, and there are only so many photos of forty-something women pouting (or suffering the effects of drinking vinegar?) that I care to see. Dating in your forties isn't straight-forward, particularly for single parents where even finding a mutually suitable time to arrange to meet can be difficult. One of the things that has shocked me is just how many women with children have ex-partners that see their children very little if at all, and through the father's choice. No love is more special than the love between a parent and child and walking away from that is something that I can't get my head around at all. Seems Candi Staton knew what she was talking about, the women keep the babies while the men have their fun wherever they can find it.

Who knows what the future holds? Being single has its plus points but ultimately I know what I want. I don't need a relationship to make me complete – I'm complete as it is (and for any Blankety Blank fans out there, by all means fill in the blank – 'I'm a complete . . . .'). But for me, life is richer when it is shared with someone special, with somebody that you know will be there for you no matter what, somebody with whom you can share both the good and the bad, growing closer through each. Somebody to whom you can give the very best of yourself.

One thing I've learned – this can't be rushed. It will happen in its own good time and in the meantime I'm striving to learn the things that this – my longest period of adult singledom – has given me the opportunity to learn. Lessons about myself, about what I want in life, and what I want in a partner. And whilst doing so, to appreciate the virtue of patience and of allowing things to happen when the time is right.

A VERY MODERN MALADY: ONLINE DATING FATIGUE

Dateline: 1 year 6 months post-separation

Okay, I'm tired of dating, we've established that, but perhaps I should explain a little more for those of you that haven't had the opportunity to step onto the dating treadmill.

For me, dating is a means to an end and that is a long-term relationship with someone that will take a special place in the life of me and my children. So far so obvious. Or maybe not, because not everyone approaches dating with the same intention. Some people might not even be sure of their intentions, whereas others may be single-mindedly clear in their intentions but less than clear (read: honest) in expressing them.

Clearly, wanting the same things out of life – well, more or less anyway – is an important basis for a successful relationship. And this is one of the many hurdles to be cleared on the way to finding a successful match. A useful starting point is to be honest about why you're dating; still, it seems the potential for mixed messages is ever present. When trying to find a match online it never fails to surprise me when women highlight their intention as 'casual dating' and/or 'nothing serious' – fair enough, we all know where we stand – accompanied by a suggestive photograph – for example, lying on a bed in lingerie – and then proceed to use the space given to describe themselves to state, in a very no-

nonsense manner, that they are not interested in one-night stands or men that are only after one thing. Hmmmm, maybe a little self-awareness wouldn't go amiss.

From knowing why you're dating we now consider what you're looking for. When looking for dates online, clearly looks are an important factor. Some bemoan the seeming 'shallowness' of discounting somebody based purely on looks and I am more than aware of the fact that you can grow to find someone attractive over time through getting to know their personality; many relationships begin this way and indeed I've experienced this myself in the past. But it's all about the medium, isn't it? As far as I can make out, people don't approach strangers in a bar with the thought, 'well, I don't fancy her but if I get talking to her we might grow close due to compatible personalities and we might end up as a couple in a year or so.' Doesn't happen. So it is with online dating, if you don't like the look of someone it's a non-starter really.

As a man aged 40+ there are certain things that are working in my favour – I have my own hair that is wholly untainted by Just For Men (have a word with yourself please, Sir Paul McCartney), my own teeth (and all of them), and I don't look over fifty. One would think that these aren't selling points but apparently on certain sites they place you in the elite class of eligibility. Add to that owning a house, a car and having a job and we're talking top percentile. Oh, and to really up the ante let's add in honest and normal. (Okay, normal is subjective and having read to this point there may be certain dissenters amongst you but what the hell, I'm running with it). Go on, Matty lad – open goal!

Or maybe not. When hearing about the standard of competition from those that are battling through their third and fourth, or thirtieth and fortieth, attempts at finding a decent guy online it can get a bit disheartening when your attempts to find Miss Right are proving futile. I mean, it's not even as if I'm one of those that poses with fish or stunned tigers (apparently these people exist, and in their multitudes) or my car (okay, okay, it's because it's a Corsa – give me a BMW and that may change, along with my ability to use indicators and not drive like an arse). And I have never sent an unsuspecting potential date a picture of my chap.

So what's going wrong? Maybe I'm just not cut out for this internet dating, I do seem to be going against the grain if the above is anything to go by. Or maybe it's just that I have been incredibly lucky in how I've met people in the past and actually a series of disappointments and non-starters is a more realistic representation of the single life. Maybe a little perseverance is needed. Perhaps, but for now I need a break. Thankfully my time on my lonesome isn't difficult to fill now that I can use it to unload/rant/whinge to my blog. Who knows, maybe Miss Right will be reading this, that elusive lady that has spent her whole life waiting for a nice, normal, decent guy that looks like Brian Cox and has a past that includes mental illness and a failed marriage.

'Matthew, where have you been all my life?!?'

In the meantime it's important to remember a few things. My brother has given me lots of good advice including the need to avoid confusing boredom with loneliness. It's important to spend time doing, or even re-discovering, the things that you love and that fulfil you. The danger is that in running from loneliness we may run into the wrong arms; as they say, the best things in life are usually worth waiting for. And in the end, despite the disappointments we may experience along the way – as another first date remains a first date, as your ex moves on and finds happiness elsewhere – we mustn't compromise ourselves by settling for less than we deserve; by believing that being with anyone is better than being with no one.

Regardless of who we meet along the way, we will always be with ourselves, and perhaps the best thing we can do when we are single is to learn how to be truly happy by ourselves, with ourselves, just as we are.

THE PRICE OF NICE?

Dateline: 1 year 6 months post-separation

'You know your problem Matthew? You're too nice.'

I've lost count of the amount of times this has been said to me. Well, I haven't been keeping count, but you get the point. How is it possible to be too nice? I like to be nice; on the whole I'd say life is better when you're nice to people. Work hard, be reliable, be honest and be nice to people – sounds like a decent recipe for a good life to me. Simples. And anyway, why wouldn't you be nice? Being nice to people, helping people, it feels good. Well, it does to me at least. So why then doesn't being called 'nice' feel, well, a bit nicer?

Maybe it's just me, but as a single man looking to amend that status, nice sounds a bit, how can I put it… Dull. Boring. Bland. Beige. And to be honest it taps into a niggling sense of myself that I've had for as long as I can remember; it goes a little something like this: 'I like you, you're a really nice guy and everything, but I see you more as a friend.'

This devastating blow to the male ego even has its own pitiful label: the 'Friendzone'. And unlike The Twilight Zone, the Friendzone isn't likely to have an unexpected twist as an ending. Maybe this isn't such a bad thing? After all, we all need good friends in life. Okay, it might not be what we set out to find when we are single but with a population of over two and a half million in the North East alone, the chances of finding that special someone straight away aren't that great. From this point of view, picking up some new friends along the way is a good thing.

'Hmmmmm, nice try, Matthew, but you still haven't convinced me, don't nice guys always finish last?'

Well, perhaps, but I'm not finished yet. Well done perhaps, a bit burned, but not yet finished. The concern that people offer on your behalf when accusing you of being 'too nice' and too trusting is that people will hurt and/or take advantage of you. That you'll be a walkover, and yes, I can identify with those feelings. As I'm sure can many of you – isn't that just the risk we take in trusting people to do right by us? By holding back, by withholding parts of ourselves for fear of getting hurt, by actively looking for reasons to withhold our trust, we limit our chances of being truly happy. Personally I'd rather look for and see the best in people, life looks better through those eyes. Yes, that brings risks, but we have something to protect us, a special power that we all have – our instinct. Our gut. How many times when we feel let down did we have a sense of what was happening, a sense that something just didn't feel right? Too often we ignore our instincts, we try to persuade ourselves of an alternative reality where everything is alright and we won't get hurt. But I'm learning to trust my instincts and they're a pretty accurate guide.

People can confuse being nice with being weak, with being a walkover, but there is a difference. That difference comes down to the value that you place on yourself, on your happiness, on what you deserve. That doesn't mean you have to be selfish, that you must put your needs above those of others. What it does mean is that you won't compromise yourself, your values, or your self-esteem in order to hold onto another. It means that you will not tolerate behaviour towards yourself that you would not consider acceptable towards others. It means not making apologies on behalf of another's actions, actions for which they are responsible. It means having boundaries for what you are prepared to accept and not accept from others in your life, not only your partner but your family, your friends, your colleagues. Remember, people will treat you how you allow them to treat you.

I like to see the good in people, I believe that most people are doing their best with the tools that they have been given, I believe that good people can do bad things, can make mistakes. And because of this I try to be forgiving, I try to understand why a person may do things that cause others pain. I believe in second chances, and I don't believe that this makes me weak or naïve. Maybe it does, but I don't think so.

What allows me to take the risk to trust is a faith, a conviction, that whatever happens I will deal with it. I'll be alright. I will learn and I will move on. And I'll still be doing my best to be a nice guy.

STUMBLING TOWARDS HAPPINESS

Dateline: 1 year 8 months post-separation

When it comes down to it, we're all looking for the same thing, aren't we? You guessed it, happiness. But what is it they say, happiness is not a destination but a journey? So far so cheesy, but as is so often the case, it also happens to be true.

We all know that when we get what we've been chasing, the ensuing happiness can be fleeting, as the inevitable question of 'what next?' or even 'is this it?' arises sooner or later. As long as we are alive there is never a pinnacle, no final destination. From the technophile forever anticipating the arrival of the next new iPhone to the Olympic champion searching for a new mountain to climb, it seems that we are programmed to be unsatisfied with our lot, to constantly chase chase chase in search of the happiness, the fulfilment, that teases us with its promise before revealing its inherent elusiveness.

When I started my blog in December 2015, I was far from happy – the sharper readers among you may have picked up on this – and I guess like all of us I was seeking my happy ending. And reader, for a period of time I thought I had it. Oh, it could all have been so perfect…

The woman that I had a relationship with following my separation had remained in my life as a friend – not the smartest decision I ever made. When she met somebody new it felt like a kick in the guts and, given how amicable our split was and how able I had been to move on from it – I was amazed at just how much it hurt. I wanted her back. I told her how I felt, laid my heart on the line, but it was too little too late – she'd moved on. There were no hard feelings but I was crushed. I cut contact, not able to stand to see or hear of her new relationship as I struggled to move on in my own life.

A month or so later, as 2016 began, she made a surprising reappearance in my life. Well, I say surprising but deep down a part of me had felt that our story wasn't finished, that unwritten chapters were waiting to be penned. And as luck would have it, with the recent birth of my blog I now had a platform on which to write them. It could have been a rom-com… boy gets divorced, boy meets girl, boy and girl split up, girl meets new boy, old boy starts blog, new boy dumps girl, girl gets back in touch with old boy… Sleepless in Seattle? Step aside Tom Hanks, there's a new leading man in town.

Except. Except… You saw it coming, didn't you? Shame I didn't. Just as the plots of Hollywood rom-coms can be tediously predictable, so too can real life. I expect that I don't need to tell you that just as suddenly and unexpectedly as she reappeared in my life, so too she disappeared. But you figured that ending at the beginning – yup, we're always the last to realise… Well, I guess life still had a few lessons to teach me.

And so I picked myself up, dusted myself down and I dived headfirst back into dating.

'Way to go, Matty, you really learned your lesson, didn't you…?'

Do you know what I did learn from this latest dating experience? That I'm not 'emotionally available'. I know, I know, I've gone too far this time. I may have just about gotten away with talking about, like, feelings and stuff over the past few months, but seriously, Matthew, what – the – fuck? You need to get a grip, son.

Well, here's the thing: post-divorce I'm finding that the dating world has its own lingo that I am still getting to grips with, and although it's a new term on me I can confirm that being 'emotionally unavailable' is indeed, to use the modern parlance, a thing. Yes, even for men (well, for this peculiar sort of man anyway). I think I'm beginning to realise that chasing after happiness, chasing after those feelings whose loss we mourn, can lead us further away from what we seek. Because in chasing happiness our feelings can be an unreliable guide, our wants and desires leading us to believe that we've found what we're looking for, turning our attention away from what it is we might actually need. In seeking to fill the void we feel through another, we may be avoiding the truth that in reality we need to fill it ourselves.

All feelings and emotions are transitory and when sadness and hurt still lingers inside, the heightened feelings awakened by meeting somebody new may mask them, but for how long? Life is a great teacher when we are prepared to learn. It is also the toughest of schools. In learning this particular lesson I met somebody new, a good person, and I hurt her. Badly. I'm sorry, and I wish I could have learned this lesson in another way, a way that didn't require another person to pay the cost.

After four years of riding a wave through the highest of highs and the lowest of lows, maybe it's time to take the foot off the pedal. To stop looking for something that is missing and instead to take in and appreciate the view from just where I am. Maybe the brightest days can be found right here.

SATS WEEK – THE SINGLES' ASSESSMENT TEST

Dateline: 1 year 9 months post-separation

SATs. Yep, it's that time of year when Standard Assessment Tests are striking fear into the hearts of children and teachers up and down the country. It's a long time since I sat an exam although I have faced a lot of tests lately, mostly in the form of first dates. Yes, first dates are tests; and, like SATs, they are tests that nobody wants to fail.

It seems an appropriate time to assess my progress, so, here it is: Matthew has taken his dating SATs – the Singles' Assessment Test – and the results are in. With nervous apprehension it's time to take a look…

Reading
Matthew has trouble with reading signals. He tries, bless him, but he needs to realise that sometimes when a woman plays with her hair it means that her hair is annoying her, not that she fancies him. And when she sends him lots of messages and asks to meet up with him it is more likely to mean a) that he is a lovely guy, and she really likes him, BUT… than b) she fancies him.

Maths
Matthew struggles with addition and has demonstrated an

inability to calculate how many first dates he has had in the last ten months (to the best of my calculations it is fifteen). He fares better when it comes to calculating how many second dates he has had, although being able to count to four is nothing to boast about. He did show encouraging progress in being able to calculate this 'success' rate as a percentage (27%) but this progress was somewhat soured when he buried his head in his hands and sobbed loudly upon arriving at the correct answer.

Writing

Matthew does show some promise with writing. His dating profile contains no spelling mistakes and shows an ability to correctly place apostrophes. Whilst these are clearly important skills for the would-be-dater, they can struggle to stand out amongst a crowd of profiles that have a greater visual impact; for example, a photograph of a young stud posing next to a pimped up Citroen Saxo with his shirt off. Some progress does seem to have been made with this 'blogging' business despite my best efforts to discourage him. It would appear that revealing himself to be divorced, dumped and depressed may not have totally killed off his chances, although to be fair when a woman has a choice between that and somebody that sends messages containing 'ov' and wiv', the former would clearly appear to be the safer bet for future happiness.

Attitude & Application

Despite his lack of attainment, Matthew cannot be faulted for effort; it would not be an exaggeration to say that he has approached his work with commendable zeal. If I were to be less charitable I could say 'desperation' but in today's molly-coddling age I have to 'find a positive'. The boy's got zeal.

Practical Skills

Matthew assures me that he has advanced practical and technical skills 'away from the classroom'. Unfortunately practical opportunities have been few and far between and I cannot in good conscience give him high marks for practical skills when there has been so little time spent honing them. To use an analogy, a top of the range fishing rod is of little use in a desert.

Overall Result

Fail – well, he's still single, isn't he?

JUST HOW MUCH DIFFERENCE CAN A COUPLE OF INCHES MAKE?

Dateline: 1 year 10 months post-separation

A couple of inches – such are the margins between victory and defeat.

I really could use a few extra inches. Not many – I'm not greedy – just a couple; just two inches more and maybe, just maybe, I would cross the winning line. So to speak. Well, that's what I'm telling myself anyway. I guess it's easier to blame factors beyond our control for our failures – or 'deferred success' in our PC world – than it is to identify things that would require some effort to address.

To be honest, at this stage of my life I feel I'm comfortable in my own skin; perhaps more importantly given the challenges of recent years, I'm comfortable in my mind. That's not to say I'm perfect (select any chapter at random for evidence) but I'm pretty accepting of myself, flaws and all. All of which stands me in pretty good stead when diving into the dating pool. Or so I'd like to think.

It's said that before you can find the ideal partner you need to become the ideal partner. Errrr, thanks for that. When you're a self-confessed reject that resides at the end of Lonely Street it isn't the most encouraging advice that you could wish to encounter. From such a vantage point these words seem particularly smug and self-satisfied, words no doubt released into the world from a balcony somewhere in Italy with the sun shining, a cool breeze blowing, a glass of something chilled and bubbly close at hand, poured by an olive-skinned beauty that desires nothing so much as your total contentment. (It's just a hunch, but I'm guessing that whoever first uttered this pearl of wisdom hadn't ever had to browse through a selection of dating profiles on Plenty Of Fish. If the notion that an 'ideal partner' does indeed exist then faith in the concept can be vigorously shaken after wading through blurry POF profile images taken in various states of dress/ undress/inebriation).

Nobody gets to be single in their forties without having picked up, at the very least, some collateral damage along the way. And the painful experiences that have led us to being single can make us more selective in our tastes, seeking to satisfy a more highly refined palate. This palate won't be settling for pub grub, me old mucka. From now on, it's going to be gourmet all the way. Having lived through the broken heart and broken hopes that accompany a broken marriage, having experienced the emotional fallout and the subsequent re-fashioning of my future hopes and expectations, a mantra plays itself out in my mind – don't settle, don't settle. Don't. Settle.

Having been left alone on the shore following the shipwreck of marriage, setting sail on our next voyage of discovery can be a scary prospect. With a heightened awareness of the risk of shipwreck, we want to be sure that the risk:reward ratio is favourable and the voyage holds the promise of a bloody big treasure chest at the end of it (figuratively speaking – I'm not training my telescope on a wealthy spinster and/or a generously sized chest. Although if it happened to settle upon either then I would certainly give them my due consideration; I do like to be open-minded).

In our determination not to settle for less than we feel we deserve, in our hope to find 'the one' with whom we shall be wholly compatible, we must be careful that we don't create an impossible ideal which will inevitably lead to disappointment.

129

None of us are perfect, and if we seek the perfect partner and perfect relationship there is a danger that we can become disillusioned when our fantasies fail to play out in the emotional and practical realities of our day-to-day lives, that place where dreams and reality collide.

Some dating profiles read like letters to Father Christmas, listing every single thing that a man must possess, as well as offering a helpful litany of every wrong that they have ever suffered and wish to avoid a second, third or fourth dose of – liars, cheats, people twenty years older than their profile photo, married men… 'If this is you, jog on' (although this sort of list strikes me as being like one of those signs to 'not put litter in the urinals' – if you are a person that needs to be told, it is highly unlikely that you are a person that will pay any attention to the sign; if indeed you can read it).

In the Booker Prize nominated novel, A Little Life, author Hanya Yanagihara creates a monologue from an imagined play. In it he notes that a relationship can never provide you with everything, you get to pick three of the things that are really important to you, four if you're lucky, and the rest must be found elsewhere. Life isn't a movie and in the real world you need to decide on which three qualities you want to spend the rest of your life with and look for them in another person. By trying to find everything you will end up with nothing.

I don't have a long shopping list of attributes that I want in a future Mrs Williams. I know that she will make me laugh, that she will be honest, and that she will understand that my children will always be my first priority. Beyond that, who knows? I'm reminded of the quote from Steve Jobs on the value of market research,

'A lot of times people don't know what they want until you show it to them.'

So I'm trusting the notion that I will know it when I've found it. And following my current life philosophy of seeking to go where my instincts lead me, this seems as good a formula as any.

One more thing – those extra couple of inches. Ladies – if you get to choose only three things as the basis for a relationship, are a couple of inches really a deal breaker? Can't we allow for a little, well, wiggle room? But maybe, when it comes right down to it, some things are just too important for compromise; I could have all the wit, wisdom and wonderfulness in the world, but I guess I should begin to accept the fact that I'll never be able to compete with a good pair of high heels.

'THEY THINK IT'S ALL OVER...'

Dateline: 1 year 11 months post-separation

Living in England there are some things that you come to expect: not having a summer; scary headlines about immigrants in the Daily Mail (every day), and being unable to drive more than ten miles without encountering roadworks (with nobody working at them). And as much as we (I) may complain and moan about them, at least we know where we stand. We learn to live with it, and in a funny way we like it, because we all like to have a good moan, don't we?

Sometimes though, we just can't help it. We try to be stoical about things, try to accept that life isn't going to do us any favours and that the status quo is, well, the status quo... but we just can't help ourselves. Against our better judgement we dare to hope, we dare to dream, we wear three lions on our shirt and... Oh. Yep, we dare to get our hopes up when we really ought to know better. Reality bites/sucks/blows. Especially when it doesn't (sorry, I couldn't help myself). Ah, disappointment, my old friend, you never leave me for long, do you?

As England bomb out of Euro 2016 (to Iceland, ICELAND FFS!) it strikes me that the dating life of a forty-something divorced male can be kind of like an England penalty shoot-out: for every Stuart Pearce there is an 'I had a lovely evening,' for every Chris Waddle a 'You're a lovely guy,' and for every Gareth Southgate an 'I'd like to see you again...' And as the ball is struck

– less precision placement, more hit and hope – the crowd rises in blind expectancy and '…but I see you more as a friend.'

'He's going home, he's going home, Matty's going home!'

To be fair, it doesn't always play out that way and disappointment can come in many guises – in my modesty I daresay maybe one or two women may have been disappointed by me (no no no, not in that way) – but the end result is the same. As much as we might tell ourselves not to have any expectations, to enjoy each first date as a night out if nothing else, it can be hard at times to stop your mind from running away with thoughts of winning the championship (I thought better of saying 'getting your hands on the trophy'). So how do we cope with the inevitable disappointments that dating will bring? (Unless of course you are one of those blokes that lies, cheats, treats their women like rubbish – they seem to be doing alright for themselves, not that I'm bitter or anything).

Well, the fact is if you're going to date, you're going to face disappointment, that's just the way it is. So you're going to need to develop a thick skin. Many people will tell you not to take rejection personally; well, it bloody well feels personal. But we don't have to take it to heart, it doesn't mean that there's anything wrong with us. It just might be that she is partial to coffee and you're more an Earl Grey tea. And – it's a cliché because it's true – try to enjoy being single, it definitely has its benefits. You know what I did yesterday? Whatever the hell I wanted to. You know what I'm doing tomorrow? Whatever the… You get the picture. Fact is I know that one day I will look back at this period of my life with a nostalgic hue; with the knowledge of the lessons it will ultimately reveal and free of the doubts and insecurities of the moment, today will take on a fondness in tomorrow that isn't always noticed unless I take the time to look.

We'd all like to meet our perfect partner but it's not going to happen overnight. If we are really comfortable with being single, if we don't see it as a problem to be cured, then we're less likely to put too much pressure on ourselves and others when we're dating. And if we do get our hopes up only to have them knocked back down again? Well, we bounce back, and each time the drop is from a lower ledge, the climb back not quite so far. There isn't somebody missing, she's out there, you're just going to have to wait a little longer to find her. Or maybe she's already there and you just haven't noticed. You never know what's around the corner; and maybe there's no need to be in a rush to get there.

LOVE, BETRAYAL & DECEIT

Dateline: 1 year 11 months post-separation

It's funny how things have a way of coming together, how scattered pieces of the jigsaw neatly slot together all of their own accord. Perhaps funny isn't the most appropriate word in the circumstances, because funny is very far from how things feel. Things have happened recently that hurt as much as – if not more – than anything that has happened since my marriage ended.

I don't think I've ever really been betrayed before. Of course I've felt betrayed, slighted, hurt, let down… but I've never been out and out betrayed. Until now. Yet I'm fighting with myself to really face it because doing so will force me to re-evaluate things that occupy chapters in my story that I can't bear to re-write. Facing the truth will force me to see things that I have refused to see. Will force me to see things as they are, rather than through the pure filter that I prefer to view life – and people – through. Betrayal cuts to the very core of what we believe – about ourselves, about others. When betrayal's epicentre is our heart, the pain is visceral in its intensity and the aftershocks shake the foundations of things that really matter – love, hope, trust, respect, memories – all are questioned in the aftermath of its impact.

In its fallout there is anger. Bitterness. Resentment. They come in waves and when the tide ebbs, hurt flows; unencumbered, unchecked as the beauty that once we saw is corroded by an ugliness that we can scarcely comprehend. These are powerful emotions and they are damaging when we hold onto them, burning us up inside and charring, scarring our pure emotions of love, understanding, empathy and compassion. For it's difficult to view the wreckage through forgiving eyes.

Forgiveness... It's something I have struggled with hugely through my divorce and beyond. I've tried hard to pour water on the flames of anger, bitterness and resentment, but their low crackle remained and betrayal stokes the fire anew. How do we forgive those that cut us so deeply, and without acknowledgement or apology? How do we forgive a betrayal that is undercut by lies and deceit? Honestly, I don't know. When we feel that we are the victim of unjust and knowingly hurtful treatment, our sense of inherent fairness, justice, and goodness is trampled into the dirt. Our trust in these better angels of human nature is soiled, and often our sense of our own better selves can be spoiled in the process. What did we do to deserve it? What could we have done differently? How could we have been so blind? How could we have been so fucking stupid?

What I know for sure is that it is ourselves that we hurt when forgiveness remains out of our reach; forgiveness for self, forgiveness for others. The path towards forgiveness is a path to our better future. It's not my place to judge the behaviour of another for I haven't walked in their shoes, seen the world through their eyes, or felt the world's slings and arrows as they have. That isn't to excuse behaviour that falls short of what we may wish to hope for – and expect – of those that we care for and that profess to care for us. But really, that is a matter for their conscience, for their peace of mind.

For us, as always, there are lessons. Things that we can take away to make sure that we make better choices in the future, to ensure that we don't live as puppets handing the strings to our emotions to those whose hands we cannot trust. It's a delicate line we tread, balancing a wish to feel the intoxicating emotions of giving ourselves wholly to another, whilst maintaining safe boundaries within our own selves that cannot be crossed, cannot be compromised – we mustn't be blind to their being breached, we mustn't question our instinct when it tells us what our conscious mind, laden with fears of a painful past revisited, refuses to accept.

What has this betrayal taught me? To trust. To trust myself, as truths revealed confirm what my instincts already knew. More importantly to trust life, and to trust the ultimate goodness of the journey that I am in the midst of. Life can be a tough school and its puzzles can be long and abstract, the answers remaining hidden until we are ready to truly understand just what those answers reveal.

This week answers have revealed themselves to me without my design – random, improbable events that revealed truths that I wasn't looking for but that have helped me to paint a clear picture where previously there was a page full of question marks. Remember the ex that reconnected and then disappeared? The one that helped me through my marriage breakdown and held a special place in my heart? Well, her behaviour a few months ago all makes perfect sense now. I feel used, cheated, belittled. I feel angry, hurt, and at the bottom of it all I feel a profound sadness for the reinterpretation of what I had thought to be something special. I chose to see the best and I was wrong. But, emerging through the clouds, is a growing sense of hope. That life really does hold something special ahead for me, something that I am being prepared for, the final piece of the jigsaw that will be placed in my hand for me to slot into place. That I deserve better and that life is determined to make sure that I am aware of that.

I have been forced to face the truth, and I must do so unflinchingly until the hurt subsides and only the lessons remain: that in the end integrity and character are everything. That honesty, love, compassion, respect and decency are strengths to be held onto no matter how difficult it may feel to hold onto them in the short-term. However life tests us, these are what will see us through, and we mustn't allow anybody, anybody, to take those qualities away from us. When somebody is deserving of our heart we need to be able to give the very best of ourselves –

a comforting shoulder, the enduring truth of our word, a reminder of how much that other person is worth when the actions of others seek to persuade them otherwise. Fun, sex, excitement, promises built on attraction and need – that's the easy part. The tests of our relationships lie beyond those things, in the enduring gifts of honesty, integrity and good character; in being able to provide the things that really matter.

Time and again in my life the worst things that have happened to me have proven to be the very best. Finally, the penny is dropping. Life has given me the answers I needed to take my next step away from the past. It's time that I finally started to trust – without question – that this really is all for my greater good. It always has been.

Have you ever noticed how life's biggest lessons are also the most painful and the most difficult to recover from? Maybe that's just life's way of making sure that we don't forget them.

LET IT GO, DUDE

Dateline: 1 year 11 months post-separation

Do you know what I struggle with? Pulling a lass. Obviously.

Okay, so that was an attempt at self-deprecating humour (although admittedly the facts don't lie and self-deprecation generally reveals a lot of truth about how we feel about ourselves), but, in my defence, trying to meet someone that you are compatible with and that you can actually find the time to see, whilst juggling a busy job with irregular hours, and being a single parent, isn't amongst life's simplest challenges. Especially when you're middle-aged. If you're fortunate enough to have to take my word for it, take my word for it.

That's not actually what this chapter is about though. No, what I struggle with is letting go (and 'Let It Go' – anybody else with a daughter under the age of ten, you know what I'm talking about). Letting go and finding acceptance. Easy to say, bloody difficult in practice let me tell you. Well, for me at least, and really, I guess my writing is in large part a way for me to try and get there (and if my blog helps me to pull a lass as well… stranger things have happened, right Donald Trump?).

'Acceptance – a person's assent to the reality of a situation, recognising a process or condition (often a negative or uncomfortable situation) without attempting to change it or protest.' (Wikipedia)

Let's get a little more specific here. I'm pretty good at the 'without attempting to change it' bit. Accepting the reality of a situation is something (I think) I do pretty quickly on the whole. My marriage is over? Right, I'm off, we're getting divorced. You don't want to be with me? See you later, I'll find someone that does (yeah, still working on that one). Please don't misunderstand me, I wasn't quite that blasé about it, but when I know the reality of a situation I like to try to get on with it and deal with it. You need to know when to fight and when to walk away.

I'm even getting better at doing the 'feeling it' bit. When dealing with any loss, it is advised that you allow yourself to feel all of the emotions that will inevitably follow. I haven't always been good at this, like most blokes there's times when I've put a lid on it, but I've learned that one way or another these harsh emotions will find a way to make you face them. In my case this can be a slippery slope to depression and I'm certainly in no hurry to go back there, so however difficult and uncomfortable I do my best to feel it and let it pass (and anyway, numbing it with alcohol, drugs, and/or taking it out on others by fighting are really not for me; as for sleeping around, well, draw your own conclusions).

But there's a bit of 'the dealing with it' that I guess I'm really not the best at dealing with. 'Without protest.' That's where I think I hit the proverbial wall and you can only bang your head against it for so long until you begin to realise that maybe this isn't particularly healthy. Funnily enough, you might get a headache. I don't mean the initial protest born of disbelief, denial and the wish that things could be different. No, I mean the ongoing protest born of 'How could you do that to me?' And it's a silent protest, one that echoes in my head as it bounces like a child at soft play off the walls of my thick skull. 'How could she do that?' 'Who is she?' 'How did I not see that?' 'What did I do to deserve that?'

Ah, poor me, poor victim me. I don't want to play some victim, that's weak and that's not who I want to be. But inevitably, there will be times where we do feel hard done by, where people fall short of the hopes and expectations we had of them, where the behaviour of those that we love lets us down. We're only human (and so are they). No, my problem isn't in wanting to be the victim, it's a difficulty in wanting to face certain things as they really are. It's difficult to face up to seeing someone that you loved as they really are – or at least as they are to you now. In my case I find it difficult to take away the pedestal that I placed them on and I guess difficult to let go of the special place that they held within me, a place that is now just space; a vacuum. And that emptiness gets filled with... anger, bitterness, resentment.

A very wise man said,

'Holding on to anger is like grasping a hot coal with the intent of throwing it at someone else; you are the one that gets burned.' (Buddha)

It's all pretty ugly, and whilst feeling entirely justified, it really doesn't do any good. The object of your ire? They don't care, they've made their choices and are living their lives without you. And you? Well, failure to accept, failure to let go can only lead to one thing – failure to move on. There's only one person that that hurts and you deserve better. It's hard, don't get me wrong, especially after divorce and having to adapt to not seeing your children as much as you would like to. But I do want to get there. I will get there, I am getting there.

In his brilliant book, 'The Power Of Now', Eckhart Tolle prescribes the following for a healthy mind:

• **Non-attachment:** everything changes, and one way or another everything that we become attached to we will lose. We need to appreciate things while we have them and let them go when the time comes. This may seem a negative/pessimistic worldview but it leads to...

• **Non-judgement:** we need to accept things purely as they are without the 'good/bad' labels that we apply to them. What looks bad today can turn into the best thing that ever happened to us, and vice versa. To use a popular turn of phrase, 'it is what it is'.

• **Non-resistance:** we need to lose our illusion of control. When things happen we can either resist them and fight against reality or, you guessed it, accept it. Accept the feelings and emotions that accompany it and accept that the past is gone and the future is never here, all we have is now and the best we can do is accept now, as it is, and make the best of it.

You know what? I think he's right. Sometimes you've got to learn the hard way. As with many other dating site users (according to their profiles anyway) I suppose I've been studying in the school of hard knocks these past few years. I'm sure the lessons will be worth it in the end, but, bloody hell, I wish playtime would hurry up and get here.

THE (CON)FIDENCE TRICK

Dateline: 2 years post-separation

I want to talk about something that can take you a long way in life and can stop you from ever making the most of the talents that you've been given. Something that can take you around the world and stop you from stepping outside of your own front door. Something that is an essential tool to carry in your dating toolkit. Confidence. Or, as I'm going to refer to it a little later, (con)fidence (bear with me, I promise I'm not going to disappear up my own backside).

To all outward appearances you could say I'm a pretty confident guy. I talk a lot (and loudly), I'm not shy in offering my opinions and will defend them as necessary. At work I have had to deal with people from all backgrounds and levels of society, from hard men from tough estates to Chief Executive Officers and world champions. I've delivered talks and presentations to local organisations and national Boards and have even enjoyed giving two best man speeches. Oh, and I regularly spill my guts all over the internet (and now in a book). I'm not what you'd call a shrinking violet. Yes, on the whole I'd describe myself as a confident person. Or, perhaps more accurately, 'confident but...'; because at this stage in the dating game, and the game of life, I'm all too aware that confidence can be a strangely fickle and fragile ally, vulnerable to a single hammer blow or to the repeated tapping at a single pressure point over a prolonged period of time (i.e. still being single after around eighteen first dates). A couple of hammer blows spring to mind, events that shattered my confidence into a million sharp shards, each one piercing my self-belief until it drained out of me and pooled on the floor.

Divorce. When the person that knows you better than anybody, the person that has sworn to spend their whole life with you, decides that they would rather be without you and is prepared to change your children's lives forever in order to do so... well, it doesn't exactly puff out your chest. Less 'Hello ladies!' more 'will I ever meet a woman again? Ladies? Ladies!?!'

Depression. It is staggering just how much of you depression can take away, or at least bury so deep inside that Indiana Jones would struggle to dig it up again. Confidence? Errrr, I don't think so, pal. When the prospect of a friendly chat with a colleague fills you with absolute, pure, unadulterated terror at the thought that they will find out just how utterly, contemptibly incompetent you are, you can kiss goodbye to the thought of ever achieving anything worthwhile ever again. (PLEASE REMEMBER: if you are experiencing any of these thoughts yourself, depression is a liar, a bloody good one no doubt, but a damn liar all the same).

These are pretty extreme examples and both instances required an awful lot of gluing and rebuilding. Which is where (con)fidence comes in. I've never been one for blind confidence, for me confidence has always required a firm basis and this basis can be built from a number of sources – past experience, self-perception, feedback from others, preparation and application. But there are other ingredients too, crucial ingredients that all of those that have achieved greatness will recognise – doubt, fear of failure, and the ability to fake it.

Boxers are a great study in this. Carl Froch carved out a reputation as perhaps Britain's toughest fighter of the last fifty years, time and again facing the biggest challenges and putting his reputation – and physical wellbeing – on the line against the best that his division could offer, often heading into the lion's den to do so. All the while he never betrayed a moment of doubt. So I was amazed to discover that as an amateur he was often beset by nerves and anxiety and required a lot of encouragement to believe in himself.

George Foreman ruthlessly hammered the great Joe Frazier to the canvas six times in less than six minutes, yet this fearsome brute of a fighter has confessed that during his intimidating stare down he was hoping Frazier didn't look down in case he saw his knees shaking.

'(Con)fidence: the ability to bury doubt beneath discipline, fear beneath faith, and fake it until you make it' (Source: me).

There are a lucky few that are born confident, that burst forth into the world and proceed to march determinedly to the beat of their own drum, to hell with what anybody else thinks. For the rest of us we need to work at it. And we can, just ask Carl Froch.

For me the knocks that I have taken in life, while undoubtedly leaving their mark, have also shown me just what I'm capable of enduring. This is a huge source of strength and of confidence and has helped to instil an attitude, and an increasingly firmly held belief, that whatever happens, one way or another I will deal with it. This belief helps to overpower one of achievement's greatest adversaries – the fear of failure. We will all fail, undoubtedly, perhaps repeatedly. But so what? Without failure there is no success. Without defeat there can be no victory, and without setbacks there can be no comebacks.

After approximately eighteen first dates (at this point I've lost count, really) there WILL be a nineteenth. Hell, there might not even have to be a twentieth. How's that for confidence?

THE ULTIMATE STYLE & DATING FIX PART 1: STEPPING UP MY DATING GAME

Dateline: 2 years post-separation

Well, I wasn't expecting that…

By now you know that my life has been pretty eventful this past few years (yeah, that's one way of putting it). There have been a number of unexpected benefits to beginning a blog, in particular the people that it has brought me into contact with. A life turned upside down can certainly turn out to have its advantages. Still, I wasn't expecting that.

It all started rather innocuously, as things often tend to. I noticed a twitter profile that belonged to 'a dating savvy alpha female' and so I jokingly referred to the fact that maybe I wasn't quite as dating savvy as I would like to be (errrr, obviously, you read my SATs results, right?). Anyway, after a little back and forth, I received a direct message:

> *'Hello Matthew, I'm loving your blog. I am just launching a Style and Dating Consultancy. I would love to have you as a guinea pig! Would you be interested in experiencing my new signature programme 'The Ultimate Style & Dating Fix' – complementary of course! Let me know if you are interested and I will send you more details.'*

Hmmmm, let me think about this…. Hell to the yes!! Maybe it's time to switch up my dating game, maybe the pupil is ready and the master has appeared? Interest suitably piqued I awaited the further information.

It gets better. It turns out that the person behind this venture, named 'TranslateHer', is Paula Williams and she has some serious credentials: over fifteen years' experience as an Image Consultant and Personal Shopper and she has worked as a stylist for film and television. The programme that I will be embarking on promises to, amongst other things:

- Sharpen up your hairstyle and grooming
- Offer wardrobe advice
- Develop your own personal style, build confidence and attract your ideal woman
- Create the perfect dating profile
- Confidence boost with Practice Date and Post-Date Analysis

Okay, sign me right up. My first task is a questionnaire to provide some background ahead of our first Skype consultation. Sounds straightforward.

'How would you describe your personal style?'
Errrrrrrmmmm.

What do you think works for you in your current style?'
Errrrrrrmmmmmmmmm.

'Do you have a wardrobe style for dating?'
Errrrrrrrrrrrrrrmmmmmmmmmmm. I have a couple of Hugo Boss tops?

Maybe they do things differently in London. Or maybe I'm just clueless. You can only do your best, can't you? So, I do just that and promptly send my responses. Next task is to send my online dating profiles over and set up an initial Skype consultation.

Apparently I have 'lots of potential'. Which I guess could be a euphemism for 'low benchmark' but best to stay positive.

So, the consultation. I'm guessing you haven't had one of these before so let me give you a brief summary of the ninety minute session: brutal. Okay, I exaggerate, it wasn't that bad. Actually it was pretty good. No, in fact it was really good. Very instructive. In short, my dating profiles are generic and boring (a surprise to her as she thought the one thing she wouldn't have to advise me on is how to write well, oops) and I completely undersell myself. Which I guess is a positive that gives me plenty to work on. And get to work we will, as we pull apart my dating profiles, rebrand Matty and launch Matty V2.0.

Easy now, ladies…

THE ULTIMATE STYLE & DATING FIX PART 2: BANG ON TREND

Dateline: 2 years post-separation

When it comes to dating, the fun part is usually when you get to take your clothes off. Turns out though that Jermaine Stewart was right. It's part 2 of Matty's Makeover – operation 'Fix Up, Look Sharp' – and I hadn't realised I could have so much fun putting clothes on.

The setting is Stratford's Westfield Shopping Centre where I meet with Paula of TranslateHer for a glass of champagne before the serious work of sorting out my (lack of) style begins. Over the bubbles we discuss my parameters and I'm given the opportunity to lay my non-negotiables on the table. Please, get your minds out of the gutter. Once satisfied that I won't be sent home a) looking like a ponce, or b) as if I am tragically denying my age and auditioning to join a boy band, we drain our glasses and set forth to leave the old (old) Matty behind and stride boldly towards some new threads. Well, as boldly as it is possible to stride in the hive of indifference to personal space and careless disregard for manners that is London's largest shopping centre.

The timing of this opportunity couldn't be better: next week I fly out to Berlin on my holidays and, before I know it, I am learning a new language, a language that will help me to navigate my way through the unexplored avenues that I shall soon be treading. But learning to speak a new and unfamiliar language isn't easy. Nein. Cut, shape, longer slimming lines, texture, layers, structured boat shoes – ich verstehe nicht (loosely translated – I haven't got a clue, pal). Still, I pick it up as we go along and Paula picks up garment after garment after garment for me to try on with the aim of transforming my 'boyish' appearance into something more sophisticated. I am assured that when she's through with me I will be 'Bang on Trend'. I hear ya, sister.

As the language barrier is being broken down, physical barriers to our progress arise, in the shape of, well, my shape. The long and short (mainly short) of it is as follows: short legs; chunky thighs; small frame; middle-age spread, and I gots booty. The middle-age spread is largely dealt with via layering and dark blues and blacks; the lower half, in particular the 'junk in the trunk' (thanks) takes a little more work in trying various sizes and styles – the 'shallow crotch' does NOT work for me – before finding a snug fit that complements my shape and doesn't make me look like Yosemite Sam.

Three hours later (and wallet considerably lighter) we're done; the result, a new 'capsule wardrobe' (a 'collection of a few essential items of clothing that don't go out of fashion, which can then be augmented with seasonal pieces' apparently). They say that every day is a school day – this was certainly an education for me and, it must be said, a very enjoyable one. It showed me that the old cliché is true: getting smartened up and looking good ultimately isn't about trying to impress anybody else. It's about feeling good about yourself, putting that spring in your step and adding that little bit of swagger that comes with greater confidence in yourself; in not being as conscious of the way other people may judge your appearance – obviously a big part of dating – because, damn, you lookin' good!

And so the unsuspecting dating pool awaits as the new, smooth, polished Matty V2.0 enters the waters, with a makeover of clothes and dating profiles giving, according to Paula, the appearance of 'fresh meat'. Make sure you bring your knives and forks, ladies.

THE ULTIMATE STYLE & DATING FIX PART 3: BACK IN THE GAME

Dateline: 2 years 1 month post-separation

Well, Paula's work with me is done, so how did I do? Has this raw material been transformed as if by alchemy into dating gold? People, read on...

I really didn't know what to expect when I started working with Paula and I learned an awful lot, more so than I would have imagined. Through a series of informal Skype conversations I reached a number of realisations that lit a series of lightbulbs in my head; hell, some nights my brain lit up like Blackpool illuminations (but slightly classier and a little more cultured, obviously). This made a big difference to me and really changed my attitude towards dating. I liked that the tips and advice that were offered weren't presented as some sort of dating 101, rather advice and forthright observations followed the natural flow of conversation and were responsive to what I happened to be banging on about at that particular time (and we had a laugh which is always a bonus).

So, what did I learn? Well, I learned that my dating profiles were boring. Cheers. The upside is that apparently they were not reflective of who I am and what I'm like. Which was nice. My first homework task was to write a profile that was me and that conveyed some of the bags of personality that were dying to be unloaded on the unsuspecting female dating populace. Okay, captain, I'll give it a shot.

Profiles suitably updated, I sent them to Paula for critical approval; a few judicious edits later (apparently I wrote too much when we were aiming for shorter and snappier; who'd have thought?) the final versions were ready to drop into dating cyberspace like a fresh meat missile.

Next, Matty, we need to sort those photos out. Apparently I look better than the photos that I was using. Personally I'm pretty clueless as to what is a good photo of me (although there are plenty of bad ones about that I have no problem spotting) and this objective opinion from a self-confessed alpha female was pretty useful. New photos? Check.

New profiles uploaded, it was time to put them to the test; casting myself back out into the dating pool hoping for a bite. And… They bit! To be honest I was surprised just how much difference these steps made to the interest that my profiles received. I was a little sceptical about some of the flourishes added by Paula, worried they would appear a bit, well, cheesy. But it seems that's why she's a dating expert and I'm but an apprentice. In fact a number of women contacted me commenting specifically on the bits she'd added. Stage 1, job done.

Of course, having a good profile is one thing but that's just a foot in the door, a toe in the water. It's all about the date and to be honest I had become pretty dispirited with dating and that's where a reminder of certain dating truths came in handy. Yes, it's a numbers game and a process of elimination. Chances are that you will have to meet at least a few people before you meet somebody that you would like to begin dating with a view to it going somewhere. And yes, it is a game – a numbers game, the dating game – and it can be helpful to approach it as such in the sense of it being something to be enjoyed without putting too much expectation into it. Each date takes you closer to meeting the person that you are looking for and even bad dates can teach you things that will prepare you for meeting her, teaching you more about the things that light a spark in you, as well as those that don't.

Perhaps most importantly, working with Paula helped me to recognise patterns in my relationships that highlighted why those relationships weren't right for me. In doing so it helped me to recognise what it is that will feel right and made me much more positive and proactive in seeking it. It also made the inevitable setbacks that much easier to brush off. I want to meet someone that feels like my best friend, that makes life fun and that brings out what I believe to be my best qualities. Regardless of any literal or practical dissection of the notion, I want to meet somebody that makes me feel like I have found a soul mate. My ideal partner who will tickle my funny bone, tantalise my mind, touch my heart and tease my... ahem.

You know what? I want something that's fucking amazing. I want to wake up every morning grateful for how fortunate I've been to meet somebody so wonderful. In the words of The Stone Roses, 'I wanna be adored' and I want to be able to give the very best of myself. Okay, I don't want to make a tit of myself about it but you get the picture. Yeah it may be cheesy, but sometimes cheesy is good.

Fucking amazing doesn't happen overnight, but I think it's worth waiting for. I have an opportunity to find it and I'll be damned if I'm going to settle for less. That's the biggest thing I've taken from this process: the road may be bumpy but the destination will be worth it and I'm headed in the right direction.

It's all well and good talking about what I've learned but let's be honest, there's a bottom line here, isn't there? Does the Ultimate Style & Dating Fix work? Well, I may be knocking on a bit these days but there's still some gas in the tank it seems, and working with TranslateHer has definitely revved my engine. And... I'm in the early days of dating the most beautiful woman I've ever met. So yeah, it's pretty, pretty, pretty good.

TOO GOOD TO BE TRUE?

Dateline: 2 years 1 month post separation

New mail: Evangeline sent you a private message...
'I love casual dating, quickies in the park and pool sex. I'm not too picky about guys so just message me and let's have some fun!'

Finally the crucial ingredient, the X Factor that I've been searching for arrives via my inbox. 'I'm not too picky about guys...' At last, my type of woman! What's that you say, sounds too good to be true? Way to burst my bubble, thanks a lot.

Upon further investigation it would seem that I have around 500 or so similar messages from young women that have just broken up with their boyfriends and aren't looking for anything serious, all of whom have seen my profile on Facebook and would like to have some fun with me. Maybe it's right what they say, if it seems too good to be true it probably is. But what if the saying isn't right?

It seems to me that there can be quite a bit of fear in the – dare I say it – middle-aged dating market. Men and women hurt by past relationship break-ups, by disappointments and let-downs, by promises and punctured hopes, leaving them closed and guarded to protect themselves from further hurt. Of course this is understandable but is it for the best? Now, I know as well as anybody that a rhino-hide can be a considerable asset in the fickle world of internet dating, where hopes can be raised and dashed

154

with the frequency of a summer downpour. Dealing with such frequent disappointments is not for the faint of heart and some form of caution and self-protection is probably wise, particularly in navigating the shark-infested waters where liars and time-wasters can be known to hunt for their latest piece of chum.

The problem as I see it comes when we begin to doubt that we really will find what we are looking for, the happiness that we seek and the love that we deserve. When we fail to fully open ourselves to their possibility for fear of the vulnerability that it would expose. When we believe the idea that something that seems as though it could be amazing is most probably too good to be true. Sometimes, inevitably, it will be. But sometimes it won't. Every day people experience amazing things in their lives. People – normal people like you and I – win the lottery, claim Olympic gold medals and overcome insurmountable odds to take their lives to a higher plateau. Why not us?

I recently heard an interview on the subject of songwriting given by Pulp's marvellous frontman Jarvis Cocker, in which he made the following observation:

'I think that's the main thing you've got to get over, to think 'I could create things'. You tend to think it's just the superbeings who can do that, or geniuses, and that's rubbish. That's what I appreciate when I listen to songs, that another human being did that, and it came from nothing. They wrote something where there was nothing before. That's kind of a miraculous event for me and that is what keeps me doing it, it's nice to have little miracles in your life, isn't it?'

I think there is a wider lesson here: amazing things don't just happen to superbeings and geniuses, they can happen to any of us, and nothing feels more amazing than a deep connection between two human beings that love each other. Further, that can inspire us to even greater things, witness as an example the great songs that have been inspired by the love for a muse (Something by George Harrison/The Beatles – I'm looking at you). But to fully experience that, to be fully alive to the possibility, we must recognise the opportunities that life presents to us and then embrace them with everything that we have.

Having experienced two bouts of severe and debilitating depression, I have experienced darkness beyond anything I could have imagined; having come through the other side perhaps my greatest realisation was that if it was possible for life to be so dark, so terrible, then it was possible for it to be brighter and more amazing than I could ever have imagined too. So it has proved to be: my job, my children, my writing – in so many ways life has been better than ever before. Yes, I've suffered further pain and hardships, none more so than divorce, but that's life. Life will hurt, no matter what we do to try to protect ourselves; but in the grand scheme of things, in the wider expanse of our life, most of our hurts are fleeting. Let's not deny ourselves the happiness that is out there for us through fear of dreaming, fear of somehow 'jinxing' what could be a good thing by daring to hope, or by deeming ourselves incapable or unworthy of receiving life's greatest gifts.

There are no guarantees in this life but whatever happens, you can deal with it. That's what people do. Take your chances of happiness where you find them and don't give yourself any reasons for regret. After all, it's nice to have little miracles in your life, isn't it? Don't hold back, don't live life half-heartedly. It may be the only one you get.

YOU CAN'T ALWAYS GET WHAT YOU WANT

Dateline: 2 years 2 months post-separation

This calls for a little context: remember the most beautiful woman I'd ever met that I mentioned a few chapters ago? I asked if it was too good to be true. It was...

Father Christmas has a lot to answer for. Every year for a number of years when I was growing up I would ask for a snooker table. Every year the genial, generous Mr Claus would fail to deliver. Well, that's harsh; he was always very kind to me – even when I hadn't been very good and had spent way too much time fighting with my brothers – and I can fondly remember many treasured gifts opened at 3am on Christmas morning. But still, I remember the one that got away; human nature I guess.

Fast forward a few years and I was discovering a bit of a talent for running and nothing made me happier than adding another medal to my collection. Looking back I see things slightly differently, noticing how many of the medals I won were bronze and recognising the lack of self-confidence that allowed me to settle for winning a medal rather than believing that I could win gold. Ones that got away? Maybe, maybe not. It's all too easy to look back with adult eyes and greater self-assurance and to think 'if only', when in reality we did the best we could with what we

157

had at the time. And anyway, I don't know the mental battles that those gold medallists fought – maybe they had no greater self-confidence than I and maybe it's all just wishful thinking. Maybe their gold medals masked their own disappointments.

Truth is, life is full of disappointments, large and small, significant and trivial, and like the proverbial rubber ball we learn to bounce back, build our resilience and try again. But bloody hell can it wear you down. Sometimes life can seem like a series of disappointments visiting our door one after the other, a steady stream of Christmas carollers banging out the same old out of tune melody, time after time after time. And sometimes we just want to turn them away and close the door for good. Bah, humbug! But we can't stop them knocking. Sooner or later we need to answer the call again.

Life isn't a series of disappointments any more than it's a series of wonderful highs, but particular times in our life may seem especially cursed or blessed with a steady procession of one or the other. I'd like to think it all balances out in the end. Who knows? I guess we remember the bits that hurt the most, leaving as they do an imprint that isn't easily forgotten as our powerful instinct for self-preservation does its job of keeping us safe. As we get older, disappointment doesn't feel any easier to deal with but we do have the benefit of wisdom and experience, of knowing that it fades, lying buried underneath an avalanche of new experiences and memories; but always there.

It's a cliché oft repeated (guilty, Your Honour) that our failures offer us our greatest opportunities to learn; 'I never fail, I learn.' Furthermore, not all disappointments are failures and not all let downs can be understood. Sometimes that's just the way life goes. I guess the best we can do is learn what we can and accept the truth as we see it, about ourselves and about others. Could I have, should I have, would I have if...? Asking these questions might help us to gain clarity and understanding, then again maybe they will just spin us into an ever tighter knot of confusion.

If we can change it then we change it, if we can't then we must accept it with as much grace as we can muster and move on, however much that might hurt. Other disappointments will be waiting for us but it's important that we don't build a shell around ourselves that will impede our view of the opportunities that also lie in wait.

Life sucks. Life's also fucking brilliant. That's just life.

THE DISPOSABLES

Dateline: 2 years 4 months post-separation

We live in a disposable age. New technologies and next big things come and go in the blink of an eye. And as much as we all want to feel special and unique, people are disposable too. From the professional workplace to personal relationships it seems that the currency of people hasn't exactly reached the gold standard. On the one hand, well, that's life – nobody owes us anything and we are all the responsibility of ourselves. But really, that doesn't make it right and it doesn't make it hurt any less when the scrap-heap looms.

I generally think – at least I like to think – that you get back out of life what you put into it, that in the end honesty, integrity and kindness are repaid. Maybe that's just wishful thinking on my part, I'm certainly guilty of trying to see the best in things despite the miserable, negative stereotype that often applies to someone that has suffered with depression. Still, regardless of whether any sort of karmic balance exists, I believe it's better to be kind to people, and while I've certainly fallen short at times I do my best and I'd say the scales are tilted favourably.

Sometimes things happen that can shake our faith in the basic goodness of people, things that make us doubt our own ability to read people and their intentions towards us; things that fall short of what we feel we 'deserve'. The fact is that it's not up to anybody else to give us what we deserve, it's up to us to get it.

People are complex: a kaleidoscope of experiences, feelings and emotions that can result in a beautiful pattern, a chaotic mess and anything else in between; furthermore each eye will view the kaleidoscope differently, filtered through the lens of their own experiences, feelings, emotions and expectations. The best we can do is to shape our own kaleidoscope into something beautiful for ourselves and those that care for us. For when we are cut loose, when we feel chewed up and spat out, when we are like litter discarded on the pavement, who picks us up? Family. Friends. Those that are there for us no matter what, that do so selflessly and repeatedly for no other reason than to see us back on our feet because they care. To them we are never disposable.

If a life's wealth were to be measured by the amount of people that care for us then the last few years have shown me that I am a very rich man indeed. Life has held its share of disappointments and hurts for me but, yes, that's just how it is, I'm far from the only one and I am never under any illusions regarding how much I have to be grateful for.

I do sometimes wonder how all of this writing makes me come across to others. I know that not everyone will understand why someone would lay out this kind of stuff in public, at one time I would have wondered about it myself. I don't want to portray some poor-me sadsack, who wants to be that? But maybe that's how it looks sometimes? I don't know. The truth is I know that there is a shadow somewhere within me and writing brings it into the light, preventing it from taking hold, keeping it in its place. Part of me is scared that if I don't write I will become lost in the shadow, alone, isolated and unable to connect with all that is good in my life. However hard it might be to write this stuff sometimes, however loud the voice in my head tells me what people will think, I know why I do this and why it's important for me.

In the end, our self-worth can't be dependent on what others think of us for that will always leave us on shaky foundations. Building our own self-worth by taking an honest, unflinching look at ourselves is the only way to shelter us from the judgements of others but it's never easy and we all have to find our own way. In spite of the ups and downs I know my worth and I'm never going to expect less from others than I would be prepared to give of myself. Others may cheat and hurt us, but we should never cheat ourselves by accepting or expecting it.

BETWEEN THE BROKEN BITS

Between the broken bits I see
A glimpse
How things could have been
Between the broken bits I try
To train my thoughts not on the why
To rest, here, with weariness lie
To calm the storm and tame the tide
Between the broken bits… I hold
Faith that given time I'll know
That between the broken bits I'll see
That nothing was broken, it was meant to be

(NOT) JUST GOOD FRIENDS

Dateline: 2 years 3 months post-separation

'I think you're really great but I see you more as a friend.'

Few sentences have the power to chill the red blood of man as this ('I'm just not ready for a relationship' is a solid runner-up).

Yes, I've heard these words, yes I've heard them more than once, and no, I never want to hear them ever again. Mind you, it has to be said that these words (or some bumbling variant thereof) have also escaped my lips on occasion. I'm no Calum Best (I do have all of my own hair though, Calum) but it seems even I have left a few hearts a little scratched along the way.

It's a complicated business this whole man + woman thing, requiring as it does (at least as far as I'm concerned) the ability to talk, laugh and *ahem, cough* for hours. Even that, it would seem, isn't enough: there's 'emotional availability', 'relationship readiness' and I'm sure plenty of other terms that the average man will never have heard of but that I expect will fill many a page of the average issue of Cosmopolitan. Last, but by no means least, there's that elusive 'spark', the 'X Factor' that tells you, YES, this is the one I've been waiting for. Touchdown!!!!

To everyone that has read about – or worse, had the misfortune of having to listen to – my numerous tales of dating disaster, it may be difficult to understand just what a complicated and dispiriting business this middle-aged dating lark can be.

'Why can't you just go out and get talking to someone in a pub like the good old days and take things from there?'

Why indeed, why indeed? Honestly, I have no idea why it all seems so much more complicated these days. Nights out are fewer and farther between with the responsibilities of fatherhood and work conspiring to make opportunities for meeting someone this way about as frequent as a Sunderland AFC win. And even when there is an opportunity to cut loose amongst the unsuspecting woman-folk of North East England, most will be either pissed and/or married. Lucky for them perhaps, not so much for me.

And so to – bloody hell, here we go again – dating sites. As someone recently said to me, it may be that dating sites contain, 'loads of people that haven't dealt with their own shit' – hardly the foundation for the start of something beautiful. There are people that do know what they're looking for but aren't honest about this with the people that they meet. There is also the fact that people can be much more specific/choosy regarding what they're looking for as middle-age approaches, having had plenty of experience of what they don't want. To cap it all I'll admit, I'm picky and I know what I like. Why shouldn't I be? I haven't had my life turned upside down just to 'settle'. Knackers to that. (Katy Perry – if you happen to be reading, my email address can be found in the 'Contact & Further Info' section of my blog, hit me up).

In my roundabout way I'm approaching my point with this. Amongst the dating disappointments and adapting to being on my lonesome, I have in my life something with a value that becomes ever greater. Great friends. Lifelong friends that have been there for me for as long as I can remember. And, through my dating and blogging experiences I'm lucky to have made some new female friends along the way. Finding that elusive romantic spark can be difficult and life would be so much easier if we could choose who we could feel it with. But we can't, and that can bring challenges of its own, particularly when one party feels it but the other one doesn't. I've been on both sides of this

165

equation and it's never easy but such is life. As with most things involving relationships, I believe that respect and honesty are key, with these it's possible to become good friends with good people with whom that romantic flame doesn't quite ignite for whatever reason.

People can have different feelings about mixed-gender friendships and some are cynical about the possibility of being close friends with a member of the opposite sex without, well, sex getting in the way. I can honestly say this has never been an issue for me (I know what you're thinking – chance would be a fine thing!) and throughout my life I have always had close female friends, regardless of whether I'm in a relationship or not. I'd like to think that because of this I am able to relate to women pretty well and I feel very comfortable in their company. This has been a real plus for dating as I never get nervous about dates and know that I won't have any problem with talking and being able to enjoy a night out with a date, regardless of whether that spark is there. I confess, there is a flipside and there are times I've wondered whether my friendships with women have placed me firmly in the 'Friendzone' where all of womankind is concerned but fortunately there are a few women out there that have proved to me otherwise.

On the whole I'm not complaining. I've always loved female company and I've met some wonderful new friends who have helped me to steer through the ups and downs of the last couple of years. Friends that I am confident will remain my friends for a very long time. The fact that a romantic spark isn't present doesn't lessen these relationships, to the contrary I've found that people that I did have that spark with and that I thought were very special have proven to be only very temporary features in my life and have acted in ways that a friend never would.

For this reason I don't think of my female friends as 'just good friends'. They are not, they are good friends. Friends that I can rely on, that won't disappoint me, let me down, lie to me or hurt me. Good friends that have your back are very precious. So no,

I may not have yet met 'the one' but I have gained some special friendships along the way. Maybe I'm winning at this dating game after all.

DATING FOR DUMMIES: 9 LESSONS FROM THE ROCKY ROAD TO ROMANCE

Dateline: 2 years 4 months post-separation

Well, 2016 is coming to a close and folks, it's been quite a year. Much of it has been spent riding the dating rollercoaster so here is a round-up of some of the lessons I've learned through all of the thrills, spills and chills. If you've been there and know the ups and downs from bitter experience, may I raise from you a wry and knowing smile, if not then please take this opportunity to live vicariously through my experiences and then whisper a prayer of thanks that there but for the grace of God…

So, in no particular order:

1. Finding your level

There's a saying in sport that it's all about levels and while a minnow will occasionally spring a surprise against the big boys in the cup, on the whole the table doesn't lie and the teams around you reflect your level. Dating for the first time in over twenty years I had no idea of what level I would find myself playing at. Well, I've only gone and done a Leicester – against all expectations and amongst the disappointments I have managed to find myself playing some Champions League stuff this season. Unbelievable, Jeff.

2. Fifty ways to leave your (well, I thought you could be but apparently not) lover

It's one thing finding them, another thing entirely keeping them. Honestly, I've been blown out more times than a windsock this year. Hey-ho, such is life and as the saying goes, it's a numbers game. It does however get a little hard to take when the reasons for getting dumped begin to feel like the universe having a piss-take:

• 'I'm not in the right place for dating right now' – errrr, I'd say, I thought we met on a dating site?
• 'I'm not ready for a relationship' – thanks, it would have been nice if you could have told me that a few weeks ago when you were telling me that, errr, you wanted 'the full thing' (to be fair, maybe I misinterpreted that one…)
• 'The married guy at work left his wife for me this morning' – cool, sounds like a keeper. (Okay, I confess, my reaction wasn't quite so sanguine and resulted in a run-in with a wall that resulted in a painfully bruised knuckle for a few weeks)
• '   ' Ahhh, and then there would be the 'ghosters', because even though we are middle-aged adults apparently some of us think it better to just disappear than having the decency to just fucking tell somebody we've been seeing that we won't be seeing them again. Really, we're grown-ups, could we maybe try acting like them?

3. Sex. It's fucking great, isn't it?
'nuff said.

4. (Not so) great expectations

In my early days of dating, an approaching first date would bring with it a certain excitement and hope. A few first dates later and this childish naivety was replaced by a more worldly 'no expectations, let's just enjoy the night out' approach. A few (figurative, thankfully) kicks in the nuts later and it was 'expect the worst' territory. Timeout! As soon as dating becomes a chore, it's time to take a break; after-all, isn't it meant to be fun?

5. There's plenty of fish (with plenty of baggage)

It's true that there are plenty of fish in the sea and as a middle-aged dater I have discovered that there's also plenty of fucking issues. Amongst the terminal debris of various dating sites you will find more baggage than a Kardashian vacation and if it's smooth sailing you're expecting then you'd better think again. To be fair I've been guilty myself of boarding the dating express without checking in my baggage; not anymore, it's much easier to reach your desired destination by travelling light.

6. There's some sick puppies out there

In meeting a number of women, I've heard a lot of stories about the men that are cruising through the dating pool. Paranoids, possessives, foot fetishists, overgrown adolescents, a man that wants the special lady in his life to wear her knickers for five days straight then to wear them himself afterwards, adulterers, men that like a high heel to make an acquaintance with their testicles… No shit (although I'm sure there's some strange creatures out there that wouldn't mind that as well). When this is the competition and you're still single, it's hard not to think that maybe it's time to settle for life with a cat and a hairy palm.

7. I fucking hate WhatsApp

As we discovered in number 2 there is a dating phenomenon called ghosting and just to rub it in we have WhatsApp. I fucking hate those blue ticks, mocking me, delighting in letting me know that she was online fifty times in the last half hour and still hasn't fucking answered the message I sent three hours ago. Oh well, at least thanks to Facebook I know she's alive and well and has eaten a giant bag of Minstrels for tea.

8. What base we at?

Time was we all knew what first base, second base etc. were and we had a decent idea of how our dating was going by reaching some pretty clear milestones. Not anymore. Social media and online dating sites have made dating into a puzzle worthy of The Krypton Factor. When do we friend request our date on Facebook? Should we 'check-in' to places together? Should we like their posts/photos or will that be a bit too forward? When do we delete our dating profiles? Are we 'exclusive'? Are we in a relationship if we haven't announced it on Facebook? Do we need to discuss updating our relationship status or do we just do it and hope for the best? Considering some of these questions may help to prevent situations such as finding yourself in bed with someone in the morning and finding out that she is on a first date with someone else when you message her in the evening (yes, I told you it was too good to be true).

9. A new hope
Yes it's a numbers game and yes you will face disappointments along the way, possibly lots of them. Inevitably this can lead to knocked confidence and an unwillingness to put yourself out there at risk of being let down and hurt again – in the end only you will know when to take a break and when to throw yourself back into the fray. But know this, wherever there is disappointment there is also a road ahead of you that will lead you to somewhere better; and the light always appears brighter when you have had to emerge from the dark to find it.

BEST LAID PLANS

Dateline: 2 years 6 months post-separation

'Everyone has a plan till they get punched in the mouth.' (Mike Tyson)

In between threatening to make his opponent his girlfriend and to eat his rivals' children, Mike Tyson uttered some wise words in his time. This particular quote has a certain resonance with the divorced middle-aged man looking to pick up the pieces of his life and start again. Well, with this middle-aged man at least. Except for the punch in the face bit, in a literal sense anyway. Metaphorically speaking, well, that's a different story.

You see, we grow up and life, for most of us, has a certain shape to it; we get a job, maybe play the field a bit before meeting a partner that we think about settling down with, we date, we live together, we marry, we have kids and we live happily ever after. Until we get punched in the mouth. Actually, when it comes, divorce feels more like a punch in the stomach or a kick in the knackers but for the purposes of this piece I'll let the analogy stand. When the hit comes, we can throw all plans out of the window. So, what next? Where's the roadmap for the divorced middle-aged man?

By now you know that, for me at least, it's not been the straightest of roads nor the easiest of journeys. Building a new life, and hopefully a new relationship, amidst the rubble of a broken marriage takes levels of construction skill and degrees of planning permission scarcely conceivable from a comfy armchair in the leafy suburbs of matrimonial bliss. That great job you've got, how does it fit around the life of a single parent? How does it support running a home and paying the bills alone?

Meeting someone and dating? 'Well, you just go out like we used to in the good old days and get chatting to someone and let nature and magic take its course, don't you?' Yeah, good luck with that one when you're juggling work, being a single parent, keeping house and you don't have any single mates with the same schedule as you. And if you brave the shark-infested waters of online dating and emerge from amongst the terminal debris with both your sanity and a good catch, well, what next?

Living together? Well, I'm not there yet but it's something I've obviously thought about on those long, dark and lonely nights. When each of you have children that you are responsible for then, to paraphrase Chief Brody in Jaws, 'You're going to need a bigger house.' And, from wondering back in the olden days whether you and your partner would find it possible to live together in peace and harmony (or at least, for making-up to be enough fun to compensate), you are now faced with wondering whether you, your partner and a joint brood of little and not so little people are going to be able to gel together as a family unit.

(Quick aside – remember when you were younger and met a girl and had that bit of dread about meeting the parents and wondering whether they would like you? Well, that's nothing next to the prospect of having to introduce yourself to a teenager, an age at which biological hard-wiring is rerouted around any capacity to be impressed by anything that a forty-something bloke can say or do).

Re-marriage? Now you know that marriage isn't always for life, is it a vow either of you are prepared to take again? The spectre of divorce that wasn't allowed anywhere near your first nuptial celebrations is far more likely to hover around the perimeter of your second. When carrying scars, it's only natural to be wary of the wound being opened again. Personally I'd like to think that

I will marry again one day but I'm in no hurry to divorce again thank you very much.

The patter of (more) tiny feet? The older you get the more of a deal-breaker this becomes (unless you're Rod Stewart or Mick Jagger, but I'm guessing that if you're reading this then you're not). For many, when dating this is such an important consideration that your intentions regarding whether or not to have children can be subject to scrutiny within the first few exploratory messages (free tip: 'I'm undecided right now but I'm prepared to put in plenty of practice for making them' is not likely to win many hearts). To snip or not to snip? To reverse or not to reverse? How will I feel about spending Sunday afternoons at soft play in my fifties? These are the questions.

You know what? It isn't that bad. Yes, life can be a whole lot more complicated as a divorced single parent looking for fireworks, but it's also a time of great personal growth, discovery and other such self-help clichés. And there's not many better feelings in life than meeting somebody in your middle-age that makes you feel like a teenager again (but with a little more experience and wisdom to counterbalance the hormones. Maybe). For all the pitfalls, for all the challenges, I maintain a faith that everything will fall into place, that there is a person I was supposed to find that will take my life in a new direction leading to the destination of home. And when that happens, whatever obstacles that appear will be overcome and everything will feel just as it ought to.

PART 4

DADDY:
THOUGHTS FROM A SINGLE DAD

DADDY'S RUDE AWAKENING

For as long as I can remember I wanted to be a dad. To create a unique human being who is part of you, who will look to you to guide them through life, who will always own the largest part of your heart – nothing else in life has ever seemed to be as important, as blessed, as purposeful as that.

I was never somebody with a clear plan of where I wanted to get to in life. Don't get me wrong, I've always had a sense of ambition. It's just that it never took the shape of a clearly mapped out plan. I've looked to grow and make progress through following my passions, applying myself, seeking opportunities, and pursuing them as they arise and I am ever grateful for where this attitude has led me. But I've always been clear about the desire to have children and all other goals have been shaped around this certainty. I was certain that I'd be a good dad.

It's impossible to adequately describe the experience of witnessing your child being born. As I waited in the delivery room, my daughter was showing very early signs of taking after her daddy – she was two weeks late and labour too was proving to be a waiting game. That's my girl. As I waited – and waited, and waited – I thought ahead to the moment I would first rest my eyes on my little girl and it was all I could do to hold back tears. When the moment finally came, my emotions… well, they disappeared. It was so overwhelming. The beginning of the life that I had so wished for, the moment that was to be the greatest, the proudest achievement of my life left me momentarily numb. Instead of profound, all-consuming love, the initial sense that I had upon seeing this little person, this life that I had helped to create, was that she was a little stranger.

I guess I anticipated some kind of instant recognition, an instant bond with this beautiful being whom I had imagined meeting so many times. Instead I realised that here was a new and unique life. Here was somebody so very precious, and it would take the coming days and weeks, months and years to get to know her. It wasn't what I expected but it remains a very special memory, an early realisation that parenthood is like nothing else, that it changes everything.

In those early days I was in for another surprising and destabilising realisation. For years I held the notion that I would be a good dad. It would be the thing that would allow me to be the best that I could be, to give the most that I am able to give, and I would leave a lasting mark on this earth through the lives of my wonderful children. Yep, I'd be a natural. One of my most cherished memories is of holding my daughter, my first child, on her first night at home. This was everything I had ever wanted, everything I had imagined it would be. It was perfect. Well, almost. As she slept peacefully in my arms, I grew increasingly tired and I put her into her moses basket so that I could get some sleep. She cried. I picked her up and held her. She stopped crying. I put her back down. She cried. 'Okay, Daddy isn't getting any sleep tonight.' I stayed awake and held her all night as she slept peacefully. What can I say, I was a natural.

After two weeks of little but feeding, sleeping, and being the most beautiful little thing that I had ever set eyes upon, the crying started. And for months and months, the crying didn't stop. I say crying, but really that doesn't do it justice. It is truly incredible how so much noise can come from someone so small. A cry so piercing it reaches into the ears, spearing its way through the ear drums en-route to the head where it rattles around the skull like an errant pinball. Suddenly this natural daddy wasn't quite such a natural. Having a baby was hard work. The fanciful idea that I once believed I could have been be a stay-at-home dad...? Think again, pal.

Parenthood is something that we grow into, and if we ever feel as if we're making it up as we go along, well, we are. Those difficult early months are soon but a hazy memory, and as time flies and years go by, you're left wondering just where your baby went. At the same time, they're always your baby.

We see our own parents in a different light when we become parents ourselves; suddenly the arguments, the disagreements, the frustrations that they just don't understand you – they're tempered somewhat by the realisation that they once felt everything that you're now feeling, about you. Being treated like a ten year old by my dad doesn't feel quite so bad (well, most of the time). As my children grow I try to treasure every moment of getting to know them, to appreciate their uniqueness and to be thankful for the smiles and laughter that they bring to my life every day. And, in one of the few benefits of being a single parent, now that I don't see them every day I'm more consciously aware of this than ever before.

There's no such thing as a perfect anything, let alone a perfect parent. But through everything I do my best to make sure that they know that I will always love them and that I will always be there for them. And if that's not perfect? Well, maybe it's as close as I could wish to get.

HOW GREAT DOES A 'GREAT DAD' HAVE TO BE?

'I love you, Daddy, you're the best Daddy in the world!'

Life doesn't get much better than hearing those words. Whatever we could wish for in our lives, nothing means more than that. As a single parent there is another side of the coin,

'I miss you, Daddy.'

It's always hard to hear, and I have yet to find any suitable words of consolation beyond reassurance that, 'You'll see daddy again soon.' As far as being a single parent goes, I'm one of the lucky ones – lucky being a very relative term here – in that I have joint custody of my children and share in the everyday minutiae that are among the rewards of being a parent. I guess it is to the credit of my ex-wife and I as parents that this arrangement was agreed upon with no debate or argument. It was a given from the get-go (or rather, the get-gone).

While traversing the terrain of single life and single parenthood, I've heard from people other than my children that I'm a 'great dad'. However, the impact of their words landing is a little rougher. I have to be honest, at times it can rankle. Not in a personal way – it's intended as a compliment and is accepted as such and I wouldn't be so graceless as to throw a compliment back in somebody's face – but it kind of niggles nonetheless. It seems to me that when it comes to parenting, the expectations that society carries are laden overwhelmingly on mothers. At every step, from pregnancy to birth and beyond, a mother's choices are questioned and scrutinised far more than a father's. Natural birth or C-section? To breastfeed or not to breastfeed? To work full-time, part-time or to be a full-time mum? To buy prepared baby food or to make your own? The list goes on, and with the answer to each question comes the inevitable weight of judgement. Judgement that seems to evade fathers.

This becomes very apparent as a single father where the very fact that you actually want to spend as much time as you can with your children and share in their upbringing (you know, fulfilling your responsibilities) marks you out as a 'great dad'. This prevailing social attitude of giving credit to fathers for something so basic is unfair both to men and to women. Within such a culture, women are laden with unfair, 'Superwoman' levels of expectation, while men are expected to be well-meaning, bumbling incompetents who deserve a round of applause for managing to wipe the right end (presuming of course that they would actually dare to attempt to change a nappy in the first place). As a single dad who shares custody of his children, I don't feel I'm doing anything special. On the contrary, I can't conceive of any reason why I would accept any less than that. Maybe I'm in a minority; if my conversations with single mothers are anything to go by then I definitely am, as I am staggered by the amount of men who choose to spend as little as one or two evenings per week with their children. Some see their children even less than that.

Surely, surely the least that our children can expect of us is that we are there for them, a constant physical presence in their lives. I don't doubt that the majority of parents love their children but love isn't enough. Loving our kids is easy, it's hardwired into us; but love is more than a feeling, it's an action repeated in the small things we do each and every day. Love is a good feeling, but many of the actions that love requires of us don't feel good, at least not while we're doing them. Love requires sacrifice; it can be unpleasant, tedious, repetitive, and, frankly, a pain. There's a name for this: parental responsibility, and this applies to fathers every bit as much as it does to mothers. Our social expectations ought to reflect that.

I said that we owe our children our physical presence but that isn't enough. In today's technologically connected world there is a danger that children are at increasing risk of losing out on the one thing they want more than anything else from their parents: their attention. Young children in particular are attention junkies with a need for an audience that could humble a Kardashian. There are few scenes as indicative of increasingly normalised contemporary parental neglect as the one that played itself out next to me while eating a pub meal this week: a two or three-year-old boy's futile attempts to pry his daddy's attention from the screen of a mobile phone. For an hour this child climbed, kicked, and craved recognition; he succeeded in getting the attention of everybody but the one person that mattered to him.

I'm not perfect and my parenting routine (routine, ha!) is far from a well-oiled machine. I can be snappy, and I overuse questions such as, 'How many pairs of hands does Daddy have?' and, 'How many things can Daddy do at once?' I've been asked on more than one occasion why there is no clean underwear in the drawers, and like most of us I've been guilty of devoting too much time to my tablet. But still, I'm a great dad, you know. Actually (my daughter's current word of choice), it doesn't matter if you know. What matters is that my kids know. They don't think I'm great because I see them once a week and tell the world how much I love them on Facebook, but because I am a stable, constant, and loving presence in their lives.

They can, and should, expect nothing less. Neither should we.

WE COULD BE HEROES

My house is home to various superheroes. I have a six year old son and superheroes hold a particular fascination for little boys, a fascination that I would suggest endures in big boys too. (Superman is my particular favourite, in case you were wondering).

My son's hero of the moment is Hulk, in all his muscular green glory. As fathers, I guess we all want to be a hero in our children's lives. Okay, I'm not muscular, I don't have superhuman strength, and I'm not green (so I'm not going to lose sleep about that one). I have managed to split two pairs of trousers in recent years, although sadly this was due to an expanse of added girth rather than muscle...

Anyway, back on topic – there can't be many better things in life than being a parent to young children during those formative years where you are infallible, the all-knowing source of all the world's knowledge; of love, security, tickles and inappropriate but funny escapes of gas. These are precious years; years that pass too quickly as your little ones speed towards adulthood and the ever increasing awareness that their parents are fallible. What I never wanted, nor expected, was for these years to be punctuated by my second spell of severe depression.

This morning, as I packed my son's plush Hulk ready for a bedtime reading session at school, the thought struck me that Hulk could act as a rather appropriate metaphor for depression.

According to Wikipedia, Bruce Banner;

'...physically transforms into the Hulk under emotional stress and other specific circumstances at will or against it; these involuntary transformations lead to many complications in Banner's life. When transformed, the Hulk often acts as a dissociated personality separate from Banner.'

As someone that has suffered with depression, this has a familiar ring to it. Mind you, I can't say that I looked or felt very Hulk-like in my depressed state. I was less Hulk, more... Husk.

Husk: A person who has no substance, personality, character or knowledge. An empty shell of a human.

An empty shell of a human. Wow. That hit home. So let me introduce you to The Husk:

'Ladies and gentleman, let's get ready to...
sink into a pit of hopelessness and despair.'

Hmmm, doesn't exactly trip off the tongue, does it? I might need to work on that a bit.

What form did my transformation take? Some people are very good at hiding their depression, I wasn't one of them. Whilst not as obvious a transformation as from Bruce Banner to Hulk, the transformation from Matthew to Husk was plain for all to see, and hear, because one of the most noticeable things about me is that I tend to talk. A lot. And loudly. Well, not when I was depressed I didn't. It took all of my effort to string a coherent sentence together.

In terms of physical appearance there were also glaring signs, like the almost physical impossibility to smile. It was as if gravity were doubling its efforts, pulling my shoulders and facial features towards the floor. And if, with some considerable effort, a smile were to creep across my lips, then the eyes were a dead give-away. It is said that the eyes are the windows to the soul and as the shadow of depression fell upon my soul, these windows became clouded and misty. Look away please, there's nothing to see here.

Now that I am recovered I have no shame in admitting my depression. In its unforgiving grip however I wished to hide myself and my illness away from the world. Without this possibility my children got to see a very different Daddy. Superman had left the building. I expect we all fantasise about being a superhero sometimes, but even Superman has kryptonite. As parents we wish to shield our children from the harsh realities of the world for as long as we can; sometimes any choice in the matter is taken away from us. At such times it is easy to beat yourself up (it's what a depressed person does most of the time) for failing to protect them, for exposing them to the painful struggle that life can sometimes become.

But, like in any challenging situation, there is also an opportunity. We get to show them that adversity can be overcome. That pain will pass. That life is not about never getting knocked down, it is about how you pick yourself up to go an extra round. And maybe learning that Daddy isn't a superhero has laid a solid foundation for greater lessons; in overcoming adversity, in enduring through times of struggle, and in recognising the importance of our family in helping us through our dark nights of the soul.

REDEFINING FAMILY

Belief. It's one of the most powerful forces that there is. People will kill for their beliefs and people will willingly die for them. Our beliefs, about all manner of things, shape the way that we see the world and our place in it. Our relationships with others and our relationship with ourselves will reflect and often amplify these beliefs.

Given the importance of our beliefs in defining the world around us, it is no surprise how difficult it can be to change our beliefs, particularly those that go to the core of who we are and how we believe the world 'ought' to be. Indeed, as humans we are prone to 'confirmation bias' – unconsciously seeking and reinforcing the things that affirm our beliefs and keep us safe in a world that conforms to the way in which we perceive it to be.

Perhaps amongst the beliefs that shape us the most are our beliefs about family. I always believed in the strength of family and I grew up, like many I expect, with the idea that family was of a particular, traditional shape; you know, mam, dad and children living together in peace and harmony – okay, scratch the last bit – until the children flew the nest (whilst maintaining a long-term account with the Bank of Mam & Dad). That's not the way that things have worked out for me. Sometimes we are forced by life to re-examine and reshape our beliefs to accommodate a new world view that is completely different to the one we held before events conspired to shake the foundations upon which those beliefs were built. Enter: divorce.

Since 2014 I have been a single parent, to two wonderful young children. I count myself as one of the fortunate dads that has shared custody of his children. In the three years since my family changed forever, I have blogged about divorce and its impact and have recently been made to realise how fine the line is that I had been treading, between catharsis and allowing myself to become too closely identified with my past. Our past shapes us but that doesn't mean that it has to define us; indeed, if we allow ourselves to identify too strongly with our past, how do we truly embrace the future that has yet to be written? But this isn't about the past. This is about now, and a redefinition of what family means to me; it is about acceptance of what is, unhaunted by the ghosts of what was.

Recently I created a gallery of my family, a gallery that hangs (finally, DIY was never my strong point) on the staircase at home. The gallery contains many photographs of my children and I, and each one of them radiates smiles, happiness and love. There are no signs of the challenges of the past three years, no trace of the tears that have been wiped away. Perhaps most importantly for me, there is no remaining sense that something or someone is missing. This is our family, this is our gang and we face the world together, the three of us. Of course, there is another member of our family, and my children are fortunate to have a mother that loves them every bit as much as their father does.

Our family might not have the shape of my traditional belief but there is nothing broken about my family. Of course there are things that could be better but that is true of all families. My beliefs about family have changed but the foundations upon which my family is built remains unchanged – love, stability, and being there for my children whenever they need me. Getting to this point has taken time. There is nothing in the preceding paragraphs that I didn't consciously know three years ago but the journey from knowing to acceptance is one that must be travelled, and I didn't notice any shortcuts along my way.

On the rollercoaster journey of the last few years there have been many times during which I have yearned to regain a lost sense of stability in my life but really it was there all along. It's there in my children, in the wonderful new relationships that we have built between ourselves. Whatever happens from here on, whatever life brings our way, there will always be our family. There will always be us.

PART 5

TODAY:
STANDING AT A CROSSROADS

LETTING GO

Have you ever missed somebody
So much…
A void opens inside
An emptiness
That aches
A longing that stretches, stretches
Reaching out
To nothing
No hand to hold
No lips to kiss
No body to embrace
No smile to light up the dark
Torn between holding on
And letting go
The addict's curse
The only way out is through
No future lies in the past
No salvation lies in what's broken
So set free your heart
Let it take flight
And find its way
Home

STANDING AT A CROSSROADS

'I am not what happened to me, I am what I choose to become.'
(Carl Gustav Jung)

Have you ever had the feeling that you're at a crossroads in your life? That everything that has happened in your life up until now has been about bringing you to now? That the choices you make at this time in your life will represent a turning point? I've felt it a few times, most particularly in December 2015 when compelled to start writing about this journey.

We all face significant events in our lives, some of which will change us in significant ways while others will pass into our history having made few lasting, discernible changes in us. Sometimes it's obvious; signature moments that change our lives in an instant and force us to find a way to accommodate and eventually re-shape our lives around them. Other times our crossroads sneak up on us, our senses detecting what isn't necessarily obvious in the events that surround us.

That night in December 2015 I felt I was at a significant moment in my life, I didn't know why and I didn't know what I needed to change nor how to do it. All I felt was a compulsion to write, accompanied by the sense that that moment in time, that period of my life, mattered. Of course, every day matters and every day brings countless unknown opportunities. Each day can change our lives forever. At a rational level we know this, but, speaking for myself, there have only been a few occasions on which I have felt it. Sensed it. I felt it when I started writing, and many wonderful opportunities and interactions have arisen as a result of that moment.

Now, again, I feel I'm approaching a crossroads. A crossroads at which I can choose to repeat patterns of thought and behaviour that I increasingly realise do nothing to serve me. Thoughts and behaviours based on a desire to escape from an unwanted tangle of feelings and emotions woven from aggregated losses, an escape that likely would result only in further knots being tied. Or I can choose a different way. I can confront myself.

I've made no secret of the fact that I've found it difficult at times being alone (yeah, no shit, Sherlock). It's not a hand I'd have ever chosen to play but it's the hand that I've been dealt (and I accept the part that I have played in holding the cards that I do). Recently I met somebody that I fell for, hard. Sadly things didn't work out and once again thoughts of what the future may have been are replaced with doubts, fears and hurt. Once more I am forced to question just how much I have really learned this last few years, just how comfortable I am being on my own and in my own skin, and to ask myself how much I have twisted and contorted myself over the years to be what others wanted and/or expected me to be rather than who I truly am.

I feel I have arrived at a crossroads that I need to face on my own. Because when faced with the same difficult thoughts, feelings and emotions a number of different times, maybe the answers aren't to be found 'out there' but 'in here'. In being alone and facing what makes me uncomfortable and working shit out for myself. Nobody likes loss, rejection and hurt, but where are our feelings and interpretations about these things really coming from? What are they really telling us? Maybe it's about time I sat with some of this crap on my own, really sat with it rather than run from it and find out why I feel the way I feel, what is really driving the decisions that I make, and whether I am really living in a way that serves my longer-term best interests. This isn't some self-lacerating, 'I'm not worthy' process and I won't be donning a hair shirt. I think I'm pretty alright when all's said and done.

But still, I know that I can get in my own way, and how I interpret events in my life has to be a big part of that. It has to change.

We can't control everything that happens to us but we can exert greater control over how we respond. Sometimes in life things don't go how we'd have liked them to; no fault, no blame, it's just the way life is sometimes. And guess what, if you do what you've always done, you'll get what you've always got. To paraphrase a pretty clever bloke, responding to situations in the same way that you have in the past whilst expecting a different outcome, is madness.

> 'Insanity: doing the same thing over and over again
> and expecting different results.' (Albert Einstein)

Maybe the Groundhog Day of finding yourself in the same place with the same feelings is life's way of trying to teach you a lesson that you need – and have so far refused – to learn about yourself. Maybe when life feels stuck on repeat it's because it's your finger that's holding the button.

This is probably the hardest thing I've ever shared. Not the hardest to write – it represents my truth and as such it pretty much wrote itself (like most of the things I write). But it feels difficult to share. Why is this? Well, I suppose because it comes from a very raw place and that can leave you feeling very exposed. But I think of the fighter stepping into the ring and risking his reputation, his sense of himself as a fighter and a man in facing the fists of his opponent. Risking being knocked out, defeated and left lying unconscious and exposed before the world.

But he's a fighter – that's his calling, that's who he is – and that is the risk he faces and exposes himself to every time he steps between the ropes. And if he doesn't step between those ropes, if he doesn't choose to accept that risk, he will never become all that he can be.

This is the path I've chosen – to write and to lay my journey out there. To document the steps on the path to becoming my highest self, a summit that cannot be reached without facing the difficult moments honestly and being prepared to face and stare down the ego, with its wish to be seen only at its best. This is my truth and sharing it is a declaration of faith, of stating openly that I will use the lessons in life's challenges to become a better person without the fear of exposing myself publicly to failure; to challenge those aspects of myself that do not serve my highest good and that root me emotionally in places that I no longer wish to be. I share it so that one day my words may help others, when I will be able to look back at this time as a catalyst for living the life that I am supposed to lead and say, 'If I can do this, you can too.'

A JOURNEY THROUGH COUNSELLING

'People will do anything, no matter how absurd,
to avoid facing their own souls.' (Carl Gustav Jung)

Something needs to change and I need help to get me there. Welcome, my friends, to counselling!

I've written about how it's okay to admit that you're not okay, however, it's one thing admitting to the struggles of the past from a position of strength, as the conqueror standing tall over your vanquished opponent; it's another matter entirely admitting to current struggles and speaking from a place of vulnerability and unknowing. It's bloody hard, I can tell you! But admit it I will, because for me it is a way of exercising some strength and control at a time when I don't feel particularly strong and in control. I'm not ill, I know that. I also know that I'm not in a good place and I need to do something about it. This is a call to change and I need to heed it. Anyway, if it's alright for Tony Soprano then it's alright for me.

It feels very hard to expose myself while I am feeling so raw. I do however want to document this experience, believing as I do that this is a pivotal chapter in my life's story, a moment pregnant with opportunities to learn important lessons about myself that will shape my life over the years to come.

Telling our stories is an essential tool for catharsis, giving our experiences form and placing them outside of ourselves for more objective consideration by ourselves and others. This point is made by author Thomas Moore in his book 'Dark Nights Of The Soul'. He also notes that we must tell our stories with honesty and a willingness to avoid excuses if we are to gain the clarity that we seek. This book's title is an expression that resonates strongly with where I feel I am. According to the cover, these dark nights are not the enemy but are in fact restorative and transformational rites of passage.

I have previously undergone two periods of psychotherapy under clinical psychologists to help me to climb out from the depths of depressive illness. This time the purpose of seeking professional help is different. Perhaps the best explanation again comes from the sleeve of Moore's book, where he highlights that these dark nights tend to be viewed in society in clinical terms as obstacles that need to be overcome as quickly as we can. What we should actually be doing, suggests Moore, is honouring these fragile periods as positive opportunities to explore our souls' deepest needs which will provide healing and a greater understanding of life's meaning.

Now, I hate being told what to do. HATE it. I'm someone that needs to understand the reasons behind things. If I know why I'm being told to do something then I can get on with it (whether I can do that happily or not is another matter). It's this that's ultimately led me to counselling — I know that I need help to understand myself, to understand what's behind the thought processes and the choices that have brought me to this point in my life. I know that changing thoughts is the key to changing our experience but in order to do that myself I need to understand why I think the way I do, to help me to better understand my subsequent emotions and behaviours.

I have found an amazing counsellor to help me navigate my way through my dark night, to help me to take off the handbrake and live my life fully as who I was supposed to be; free from the insecurities and misconceptions that are keeping me stuck and preventing me from being all that I can be. After three sessions I have already gained some significant insights into my patterns of thinking and behaviour that are enabling me to make connections that previously eluded my reach. Such insights don't always represent entirely new information; rather they are presented in a particular way, by a particular person, in a particular context, and at a particular time of your life when you are ready to synthesise such insights, that somehow enables them to 'click' into place – to slot into the overall puzzle of who you are, and why you are.

One such insight explains a lot about how I've been feeling for the past few months. As is often the case, a good analogy helps to illustrate the point. The Death Star is me (bear with me here), the Death Star's Superlaser is depression. This 'superlaser' is a relatively small part of the whole, yet its planet-destroying destructive capability gives it a power and a presence wholly out of proportion to the reality of what constitutes the whole. That such damage can and has been wreaked by this weapon has left a lingering wound, a sense that somewhere inside I am somehow 'broken', or at the very least that I risk being broken again. And that my friends, is bollocks. In the light of awareness, darkness can no longer exist.

Rather than fixing something that is broken (it isn't), through therapy I am in a process of 'polishing my rough edges'. This isn't about needing to make massive changes to who I am, it is about questioning and building my sense of self, the core sense of who I am in my soul, distinct from the real and perceived judgements of others and the stories I have told myself regarding how and where I fit into the world. Jung discusses the process of telling our story in the imagery of alchemy:

'The selfish hardness of the heart is dissolved, the heart turns to water. The ascent to the higher stages can then begin.'

Moore asserts by extension that our stories are a kind of water that makes fluid the events of our lives. Our stories 'liquefy' us, preparing us for transformation and bringing forth from our dark night tales that deconstruct our existence, putting us back in the cool, clear and flowing river of life.

It is time to write a new chapter in my story, and to trust that the river of life's flow is carrying me to where I am supposed to be.

DOUBTS, INSIGHTS & PRETTY EPIC-NESS

'Out of suffering have emerged the strongest souls; the most massive characters are seared with scars.' (Kahlil Gibran)

Oh bollocks, what the hell have I done?!?! I've been hit by doubts. Doubts about sharing this journey through counselling. The things I write about are subjects that can be tough and uncomfortable and, despite having shared my writing for a year and a half now, it can still be difficult. Believe it or not, I don't have a wish to reveal too much of myself and, strange as it may seem to anybody that has read this far, I don't really feel that I do. I consider the things that I write about to be pretty universal, situations and circumstances that many (most?) of us find ourselves in at some point in our lives. Viewed in this way a more detached perspective on personal circumstances is afforded. That said, the experience of counselling is an intensely personal experience that delves into the core of who we are. Of who I am.

What I hope to do in writing about it is not spew out the guts of all my deepest doubts, fears and insecurities but rather to reveal something of the process and its value, to reduce any fears that others may have about seeking counselling for themselves. Admitting that you're receiving counselling, or are 'in therapy', inevitably brings with it the weight of others' perceived judgements of you, to which I would say, most politely, fuck that.

Because ultimately it is your life and the reality is that we all need help from others at some time in our lives, whether that be from family, friends or a professional counsellor. Nobody can disagree with that yet I expect most of us would feel some level of fear, or at the very least trepidation, about admitting it openly. And while we all have friends and family around us, relatively few of us will ever seek professional help despite the good that it could do us.

It's struck me that when I've discussed my experiences with other people, many, many of them have said to me that they have considered counselling at some point in their lives and that it is something that they believe would benefit them right now. I expect that for most people that do seek counselling it's only when the wheels begin to fall off pretty spectacularly that help is sought, being in the position of absolutely needing professional help and not knowing how to navigate life's circumstances without it. That was certainly true of me in 2006 and even then I resisted for far too long. Yet, like many things in life, once we have taken that step once it becomes much easier to do so again. At this time I am prepared to seek counselling not just because I feel that I need it, but rather because I know that I will benefit from it.

Seeing a counsellor doesn't mean that you are broken or that you are weak or that you can't cope, it means that you are human. This seems to be much more accepted in the US than it does here in the UK; indeed over there the reputation of one's therapist can compete with that of the personal trainer as a status symbol (I would recommend that a certain Mr Trump finds a good one for all of our sakes). Counselling features in a number of top TV shows including The Sopranos and The Affair, and one of the most popular TV characters of recent decades, Dr Frasier Crane, is a therapist. Counselling is difficult and it can be very uncomfortable, but then nothing worthwhile comes without difficulty. Achieving greater self-awareness and laying the foundations for a better, happier future is a benefit that outweighs any cost. That said, counselling is also very interesting and can even be fun; and moments of genuine insight offer great fulfilment.

Something that I am really learning about is the gap between intellect and emotion. I've always been interested in people and fascinated by psychology and as such have always been keen to learn about what makes people tick and why we do the things we do. I've read avidly on many subjects including psychology, philosophy, religion and biography and I have developed a pretty good intellectual knowledge of such things. However, as I've found to my cost on more than one occasion over these past few years, there is a big difference between knowing something at an intellectual level and applying things in your own life once messy emotions get involved. Like many, I seem to be good at offering my advice but much less so at taking my advice. While we can question and add to our intellectual knowledge relatively easily, understanding our emotional responses – particularly intense emotions – can be much more difficult. After all, if we feel something, we feel it, right?

Our emotions aren't right or wrong, they just are, and they are a big part of us. But we can learn to understand our emotional responses, to recognise the things that shaped our emotional development and to understand why we feel and think the way we do. Looking back into our developing years we can begin to see how and why our patterns have developed, providing us with an emotional A to Z to enable us to seek alternative routes when interpreting and dealing with events. Knowing something at an intellectual level is one thing, examining and dealing with it at an emotional level is something else entirely, something that I know I would not be able to do without the help of a professional.

Much of what we think and feel about ourselves and the world has been ingrained since we were a child, a time at which we didn't have the intellect or experience to question or understand the events in our life in the way that we do as an adult. The beliefs and emotional responses that develop through these experiences run deep and carry through into adulthood, resulting in behaviours and emotions that repeat patterns long-since established and rarely questioned. Responses that can be out of kilter with the reality of what our intellect tells us. We all have our issues and challenges and this isn't about assigning blame to anybody for feeling the way we do, rather it's about understanding it. We are responsible for our lives and the choices that we make and greater self-awareness can only help us to make choices that are better for us and the people that we care for.

In counselling we can also come to appreciate all of those things that make us uniquely us, the many great things that far outweigh the issues we might be facing in the present moment. In the words of my counsellor, I need to realise how pretty epic I am (well, she actually said epic but I'm not yet able to say it with the same conviction so I'll stick with pretty epic for now). If this sounds arrogant or conceited – something us Brits aren't overly comfortable with – it isn't meant to be. One thing I've really learned over the past few years is that ultimately while it's wonderful to have people around us that will love and support us – and I'm very fortunate in that regard – there's only one person that we can guarantee will be with us until the very last. Ourselves. You don't want him or her to be getting on your case, giving you grief and telling you how useless you are when things are tough, do you? Best to make sure that you know he/she is epic, don't you think?

So, from my doubts I emerge and here I am again, writing about counselling. I hope that in some small way this may help others to seek the help that could benefit them so much.

PUTTING THE GOOD IN GRIEF

In an image obsessed, filter-obscured and airbrushed world that prizes the 'perfect' form, the self-esteem of many is invested in its myth; deposits are made in the self-esteem bank with every unflattering snap of a celeb's bingo wings, while withdrawals accompany the comparison to toned torsos that most of us will never attain or reclaim. I'm carrying some extra poundage myself but at forty two and with various competing priorities in my life I'm not losing too much sleep about it. Indeed, I'm accepting of the fact that the closest I'll ever get to the distant glory days of being an eight and a half stone runner is in my dreams.

There's another weight that I'm carrying, and it is weight that I'm determined – and working very hard – to lose. This weight that I carry isn't visible, or at least not in the sense of a physical weight, but maybe it's been more visible on my face than I've imagined it to be, and maybe the sense of its presence has been felt more keenly by others than I have realised. As is so often the case, the weight has accrued steadily over the years, the consequence of poor nourishment. And just as too many poor food choices will eventually result in burdening the joints with more weight than they can comfortably carry, so too can a steady diet of unhealthy thoughts and beliefs come to burden the mind, the heart and the soul with a weight that becomes wearisome to carry.

Sometimes we find ourselves looking in the mirror and wondering who it is that is looking back. It has been said that our relationships are mirrors to our souls, reflecting both our brightest lights and our darkest shadows. Thus, our partners can be amongst our greatest teachers and can afford us the opportunity to discover new truths about ourselves. But even with the very best of teachers we are only able to benefit from their wisdom if we are open to receiving it. When our relationships end and the mirror is removed, we are left only with ourselves. These periods offer the opportunity to explore the truths that the relationship revealed to us, to gain a deeper understanding of who we are both within and outside of our relationships, and to incorporate this knowledge into our future decision making.

As such these challenging times can be the making or the re-making of us; times that we can look back on with gratitude for the deeply buried gold that they enabled us to mine. There's a problem though: it's hard. Like, really fucking hard. It can be far easier to search for a short-term fix than to focus on the long-term and to patiently and diligently work through the pain, sitting with it and allowing it to re-shape and strengthen us. It can be far easier to fall for the quick fix, to try to shed the weight of our loss quickly and present an apparently healthier version of oneself to the world, only to find months later that we are trapped in a cycle of yo-yoing, having failed to do the emotional detox that was needed.

When we face a significant loss in life we need to fully grieve it to fully move on from it, to assimilate its lessons and make peace with it. They say that time is a great healer but time alone is not enough. By failing to fully allow ourselves to process and acknowledge our grief, by running from the pain that it brings, we merely push it beneath the surface to hibernate until our next loss makes an unwelcome visit and draws it out from its hiding place. And don't be surprised if it has grown during its hibernation, unresolved grief can be a very heavy and stubborn weight to shift.

A failure to grieve isn't necessarily a wilful avoidance, sometimes we just don't know how to. Of course, nobody wants to hurt and it is natural to seek respite from what ails us. For these reasons counselling can be very beneficial in helping us to understand exactly what it is that we are grieving and to reveal the deeper truths that our reactions to our losses point towards. It helps us to learn how to grieve, to recognise and understand grief's stages and realise that what we are feeling is normal and will dissipate with time, work and self-care (no matter how much of a mess we might feel at times).

I've done my best to process and move through the challenges of the past few years following the breakdown of my marriage and writing has played a big part in that. However, I have come to realise that I haven't fully grieved what I have lost, not really. And I risk becoming stuck, burdened with a weight that I no longer wish to carry. With the help of a wonderful counsellor I am working through this and shedding the weight so that I can truly feel light and carefree. To be honest, it's a long time since I have felt that way for any prolonged period. But I know that I can feel that way, and that I owe it to myself and my children to be that way.

So I'm letting go of my excess baggage and placing no expectations on life. Instead I'm focusing on becoming the best version of me and on making the most of the amazing future opportunities that are sure to come as a result.

BIG BOYS DON'T CRY

Apparently us men don't 'do' emotion. Well, that's a load of bollocks, isn't it? Either that or I am totally out of touch at this point and am out of the 'man club'. (Okay, I'm prepared to accept that this could be a possibility).

Men show emotion all the time. Go to any football match (if you haven't been priced out of it by corporate greed) and you will see a whole range of emotions on display – joy, fear, anger, sadness (I'm from the North East of England where the last of these is particularly prevalent). These are displayed by players and fans alike and when stakes are high the packed stadia are often referred to as 'cauldrons of emotion'. It's far too simplistic to say that men don't do emotion, of course they do. Maybe the real issue here is which emotions are considered socially acceptable for men to show, and in which contexts they are permitted.

When we use the word 'emotional' to describe someone's behaviour, what we tend to mean is crying, upset, suffering and sadness – things that signify vulnerability which, in turn, can be seen to represent weakness. Being 'soft'. Especially to men.

Piers Morgan recently caused a stir with his comment that he was not convinced by the new trend of 'male public soul-bearing' (unless presumably it is taking place on 'Piers Morgan's Life Stories' and is good for viewing figures). In fairness I'm bound to take issue with Mr Morgan, aren't I, and not just because he's a massive twat. Let's face it, I'm not exactly averse to a bit of male public soul-bearing, am I? That said, even I have my limits.

I'm certainly no fan of the commodification of emotional pain, of the cynical exploitation of suffering and heartache or the use of tears as a marketing strategy designed to tug at the purse strings as much as the heartstrings. But such cynicism shouldn't be used as an excuse to pack our very real emotions away into some socially acceptable hiding place, because in denying our difficult, hurtful and uncomfortable emotions – those that leave us vulnerable – we deny our very humanity. And that isn't good for any of us.

I'd consider myself a caring, sensitive person. I'm not afraid to admit that I will tear up to E.T. (and so will you, don't try to deny it), but there have been many times in my life when I should have felt emotional but instead I felt numb. Times when the depth of emotion that ought to have been there somehow wasn't, in situations and contexts where tears were both socially acceptable and the most appropriate emotional response.

Family funerals are an example. I have delivered a number of eulogies and been told by people that they didn't know how I was able to do it whilst keeping my emotions in check. Of course I've shed tears following bereavement, yet on each occasion I felt that I should be crying far more given the nature of the loss. I even felt a certain guilt that I didn't. Another example is the birth of my first child. She was two weeks overdue and her birth followed a long labour. Having waited so long to meet her the very thought of her birth made me tear up, right up until the moment she arrived; when the moment came… not a wet eye in the house. It seems I would feel things but not really feel them to the point that they were emotionally expressed. I never really questioned this, I just figured my emotions were stilted in some way but that didn't matter, there's worse ways to be. Right?

A time when I did cry – a lot – was when I was suffering from depression. However I wouldn't consider this any sort of emotional response, let alone an appropriate one. At my worst I felt utterly broken inside and tears emerged from a void of true emotion, the tears that bled from my eyes formed from pure anguish and despair.

I reflect on all of this now because things are changing. I am changing. Since beginning counselling a few months ago, the work that I have been doing has unleashed a shitstorm of emotion. It's something I've never felt before and, as is my nature, it has prompted me to reflect on things. And, as is my nature, to write about them. The shitstorm has been unleashed via tearing off long-standing emotional scabs and exposing the wounds beneath. Facing, accepting, feeling and expressing these emotions is necessary for healing to take place and yes, it leaves you extremely vulnerable and extremely raw. But this, my friends, is far from soft. On the contrary this is hardcore badass terrain that is being traversed.

And yet… there's no getting away from the fact that there is a huge amount of resistance that has to be overcome to face this, and not just because it is painful. Such emotion can carry with it a heavy dose of self-recrimination, frequent chiding of our 'self-pity', our 'self-indulgence'; questioning the validity of our feelings when others are facing far worse in their lives, and often in the absence of the blessings that fail to cut through our own personal pain. But our feelings aren't right or wrong, they just are. They can't be denied any more than we can deny that Piers Morgan is a massive… Sorry, forgive me. They can be denied no more than the nose on your face. Should we try to deny them, to repress them, they will find their expression somehow, someway and at sometime. When they do, chances are it won't be pretty and it won't be healthy, for both ourselves and/or for those that happen to be in our orbit when the time comes. In fact, emotional suppression can be very damaging indeed. Denying our emotional selves the expression that we crave can be just as bad for us as denying our physical selves the food that nourishes us.

I believe that this denial of our emotional selves is compounded hugely by social conventions that are maintained by the attitudes of the likes of Morgan, and the 'stiff upper lip' mentality that stubbornly clings to the collective British psyche. With suicide being the UK's leading cause of death for men under the age of forty five, it is vital that we challenge this attitude. Thankfully there is a growing recognition of this, perhaps most notably apparent in the brilliant work being done by Princes William and Harry via their Heads Together project. Prince Harry has spoken powerfully and movingly about the repressed grief he has endured for decades following the tragic loss of his mother, and its personal cost.

Painful, vulnerable emotions make us uncomfortable. They are uncomfortable to feel and many of us are uncomfortable in the presence of the overwhelming emotion of others. So how do we become more accepting of them? With compassion and empathy, those emotions that will naturally arise when we open our hearts to the suffering of others, and ourselves, with acceptance and love instead of resistance and fear. A place from which we can acknowledge the validity and necessity of our emotion.

With empathy and compassion for ourselves and others comes the true gift of emotional vulnerability: a true, deep and authentic connection with ourselves and others. We can share our deepest humanity. In that lies beauty and love, and in our love lies our greatest strength. I'm not advocating that we all start crying into our Costa coffee to strangers on the train, but we need to feel more able to accept and acknowledge our emotional vulnerability to ourselves and those that love us. For only then can we fully embrace our humanity and access our deepest strength, and only then will we be able to live and love fully and fearlessly. We need to develop a culture in which we can be more honest about this. Recent tragic events in the news have led to mass outpourings of love, compassion and care that reveal the true beauty that is at the core of the human spirit. We need to feel able to show the same love, compassion and care towards the personal trials and sufferings of ourselves and others, for at any given time many of us will be fighting our own battles in one way or another and there is no shame, no weakness in admitting that.

I believe that my recent experiences are helping me to become a more emotionally developed, more emotionally well rounded man. I believe that this will make me a better parent and, one day, a better partner. And I want my son, my sweet, sensitive little boy, to grow up in a society where those qualities that I love so much in him will not be knocked out of him. Where compassion, empathy and true, authentic emotion can be truly embraced as the strengths that they are, alongside the more obvious and traditional strengths that we rightly admire in our sons, fathers and brothers.

If crying was okay for Winston Churchill – that enduring symbol of the British bulldog spirit and indomitable will who 'loved a good blub in Parliament' – I'd say it was alright for me. And for you too.

CARL ROGERS WOULD BE PROUD: A PAUSE, PROGRESS & A PAT ON THE BACK

'The curious paradox is that when I accept myself just as I am, then I can change.' (Carl Rogers)

I've been seeing my counsellor, Nichola, for a couple of months now and it's been hard, very hard. This is necessarily so, if the process is to be worthwhile then you need to give yourself fully to it. Just as rehabilitation from a physical injury is often a gruelling process, so too is dealing with the complex feelings and emotions that are brought to the fore in counselling. Similarly, the pain is borne on the understanding that it has a greater purpose, strengthening the parts of you that are healing.

Truth is, it doesn't always feel like great progress is being made when you are digging around in the sludge and shit that you have unearthed; sometimes it just feels that you are covered in shit. Given that, it is important to trust in the process and to have faith that the end result will be worth it all. That where you're going to is better than where you've been. As such, at this stage in the process it's important to take a pause to consider where I'm at (it's this week's homework). So, here is my very own magnificent(ish) seven.

1. I'm here

No no no, I'm not wishing to imply anything dark or dramatic here, I mean that I'm glad to be at this stage in the process. I'm not yet where I want to be, but nor am I where I was. When progress seems slow – translation: 'when you're impatient to get to where you're going' – it's easy to forget where you were a matter of months ago. And while the time can go slowly, it's really not too long in the grand scheme of things.

2. I accept that I'm here

Acceptance is very powerful and it can also be difficult to come by. So much of the past few years has felt like a battle, with much resistance and resentment towards unwanted situations and feelings. Whilst this may be a natural response to difficult changes and, I expect, a necessary part of reaching acceptance, it is also draining. I feel I'm finding more peace in how things are, a peace revealed gradually by both the passage of time and the insights that I am gaining into myself through facing my challenges.

3. I'm learning about who I am

I would like to think that I'm pretty self-aware but I've been amazed at just how many significant insights I have discovered through working with Nichola. I am discovering that there is a big difference between being aware of and recognising aspects of yourself, and in actually understanding them, in recognising where they come from and questioning whether they are in fact serving your better interests. As these insights grow, they are accompanied by the sense of things gradually shifting inside. With deeper understanding we begin to see things with different eyes. Of course, we don't shift a lifetime of thinking patterns in a couple of months, but once the light of awareness shines, it illuminates a different set of choices that are available when faced with questions about what is best for us in a given set of circumstances.

4. I'm more accepting of who I am

Sometimes I wish I was simple. Not 'simple' simple, but more able to just deal with and accept things at a more surface level. To maybe be more satisfied with the surface level, transitory pleasures of life. But I'm not. I have a questioning nature, I want to learn and know more, I want to understand things, I want my life to have meaning, I want my relationships to have meaning. I want to be the best version of me that I can be. I can overthink, I analyse, and with all of this comes a tendency to be overly self-critical. To bring the blame for things back to myself and to zoom in on those aspects of myself that may have contributed to whatever unwanted situation I find myself in. And to wish that they weren't a part of me. I'm learning to be more accepting of who I am, to embrace all of those qualities that make me 'me' for only then will I truly live the life I am capable of living, free to be who I am at my core without the need for validation from anybody else. To be who I am, not who I feel I somehow ought to be.

5. I haven't ran

A long, long time ago I was a runner, until arthritis in my foot forced me to stop. Over the last few years I've found myself running again, only this time in a metaphorical sense (my body wouldn't have it any other way!). It's natural to want to escape from the pain that we feel, to search for distractions and external cures and answers, but I'm learning that a big part of the cure is to feel what we are feeling and to sit with those things that are difficult for us. Heartache, sadness, grief, loneliness, doubt, fear, confusion, uncertainty... In counselling, I've unleashed a shitstorm of emotions as what has long been repressed has broken free, and sitting with these things is fucking hard. But I'm doing it and I'm still here; slowly, bit by bit, these feelings dissipate.

6. I'm a hardcore badass

I've been playing a tough hand these past few years. Life has challenges in store for all of us, it just so happens that this is my time to buckle up and endure a bumpy trail for a while. Whilst fully recognising that many, many people have far greater challenges than I, Nichola has helped me to see that I've been dealing with some 'hardcore' stuff that can send a lot of people under. I'm still here, and I'm okay. When I started to see Nichola, I was, as she describes it, 'frantically fighting the tide'; now I'm 'floating in the middle of the ocean' and preparing myself to kick on to a new shore. I'm not going to be pulled under again. I'm pretty damn hardcore myself. In fact, I'm a regular badass (but a nice one).

7. Carl Rogers would be proud

Who? Carl Rogers is one of the founding fathers of the humanistic approach to counselling. According to Nichola, I'm a 'dream client' and have worked hard in facing difficult things without shying away from them. In her words, 'Carl Rogers would be proud of you.' Rogers described the life of the fully functioning individual as rich, full and exciting and he suggested that they experience joy and pain, love and heartbreak, fear and courage more intensely.

'This process of the good life is not, I am convinced, a life for the faint-hearted. It involves the stretching and growing of becoming more and more of one's potentialities. It involves the courage to be. It means launching oneself fully into the stream of life.'

It's reassuring to know that such depth of feeling can be considered a component of being a fully functioning individual, rather than a somehow defective one. That being caring and sensitive is not a fault, especially when living in a world where the devastating impact of their lack is sadly too frequently observed. Anyway, if Carl Rogers would be proud of me then I guess I can be pretty proud of myself.

'The good life is a process, not a state of being. It is a direction not a destination.' (Carl Rogers)

FINDING ACCEPTANCE:
THE VIEW FROM THE LEFT

Perhaps unsurprisingly since writing about my divorce, I get people confiding in me that they are unhappy in their marriage. This, and hearing the wonderful 'Leaving' by Suede this morning, has prompted reflection on the 'other side' of the divorce story: that of the person that leaves.

Technically I guess I left my marriage, or at least it was me that left home once it was apparent that my wife had emotionally left the marriage. Since then, as you are now well aware, a huge amount of my time and energy has been spent adjusting to the unfamiliar shape of a life that was never wished for and never anticipated.

Three years on, with all the ups and downs, I finally feel able to say that this is my life and I accept it. I feel able to accept life fully as it is right now without rationalising my present situation as a single dad as some sort of transitional period between my married past-life and whatever life the future may throw at/hand to me.

Now I realise – no, I know – that there is no past-life and future life, there is just life, just now; and now is all about doing the best I can right now: what is best for my children, what is best for me. However much it might have hurt, however much it ripped apart my life, however difficult the past three years have been at times, I can acknowledge and accept that in taking the decision to end our marriage, my ex-wife was doing exactly the same thing as I am trying to do now – what she felt was right and best, for her and for our children.

When I speak with people that are considering leaving their marriage, or at least are beginning to question the future of it, I can feel torn. Torn by knowing the pain and heartbreak of being left, of knowing the damage that would be done in the aftermath of their taking the decision to leave and naturally empathising with the person that will have to face the challenges that I have faced. I wouldn't wish divorce on anybody. But knowing that there exists a happy life on the other side of divorce, a life rich in lessons and new opportunities, in spontaneity and freedom; a life in which the rubble of what was is gradually cleared away to expose clear space on which to build something new, something better, something lasting... Don't we all deserve that?

I can't advise people not to leave; to forsake the pursuit of a happiness that they feel is missing and that isn't coming back. I wouldn't wish that for myself, I wouldn't wish that for my children; we need to make the most of the time we have here to become the best that we can be, not just for ourselves but for the influence we can have on the lives of others. Only we can forge our path and decide which is the better direction for us to take, and however good we are, however caring we are, inevitably that will at some stage involve hurting someone else.

There is no pain quite like the pain of your marriage ending, especially when that involves breaking up a family with children. However much it hurts to be the one that has no say in the matter, I don't discount the pain and difficulty that must be faced by the one that leaves. Guilt, doubt, questioning, fear, sadness, self-reproach – I expect that all of these feelings would have to be dealt with and that can't be easy. I don't believe that divorce is a decision that anybody takes lightly. Facing the emotions, pain and potential backlash of making that final decision make deciding to leave a marriage a very brave thing to do.

I understand why my marriage ended and I understand the decision that my ex-wife took in calling time on our life together. If I'm honest, I don't doubt that I will have a better relationship in the future and that's not meant to disparage my marriage in any way, nor the love I had for my ex-wife or the special times that we shared. It helped to make me who I am.

So far so saintly – aren't I mature and wise and philosophical about it all? The reality of the situation is that, well, it's not that straightforward. However objectively I can view the situation with the perspective of time and experience, there are things that I'm not sure will ever sit easily or happily with me. Half of my children's lives are spent away from me; half of their lives are spent living with another man. That can still hurt. It strikes right at the core of what is most precious to me, but my children are happy and they are good kids. I do hope and believe that divorce doesn't have to have a long-term damaging effect on their lives despite the obvious challenges that it has brought. Life can be happy for all parties following divorce once the dust has settled. I expect it usually is for the most part, we humans are a very adaptable bunch.

I do believe that my life will be happier and that I will meet somebody that I can't imagine living without. It will never be the life I anticipated, the life I wanted as far as my children and my commitment as a father are concerned. Life is more complicated. My feelings can still be conflicted and the voice of my better-self can sometimes be shouted down by the sudden appearance of an emotional self that doesn't forget. And yet, I have no regrets. Of course, there are things I could have done differently, maybe should have done differently, but I did the best I could at the time. And I know that in taking the decision to end our marriage, so did she.

WHAT HAVE I BECOME?

It's one of those days. A day of quiet reflection and where better to do it than my favourite cafe in Sandsend with my obligatory pot of Earl Grey tea (milk, not lemon, I'm not that pretentious).

On days like this I am most thankful for whatever it was that lit the fire inside for writing. I'd always enjoyed my own company but it takes on a distinctly different flavour as a regular way of life, rather than as the short-lived and much savoured taste that was to be found amongst the often hectic life of a husband, father and busy employee. Time alone without someone else to talk with, mixed with a contemplative disposition, can lend itself to living in our heads. It is at these times that writing is such a gift to me.

Today I find myself contemplating identity: who am I now? Whenever I used to hear people talking about the need to 'find themselves' or 'get to know themselves' I used to find the notion absurd – how was it possible to not know yourself? Aren't you the only person that you do know? Ah, the innocence and naivety of youth. Time and life have shaken my certainty, and, reflecting on these past few years, it strikes me that there is one thing in particular that can shake our very foundations of self: loss.

When we lose things that are important to us we can also lose a label that helps to define us. Husband. Father. Sane. These labels are often laden with meaning; meaning that can form a significant part of our self-identity. As well as offering a sense of meaning, the labels that are applied to us can confer something else – status. They can come to define not just who we are, but also what we feel we are worth. And when we lose an important label we can come to realise how much of our identity, how much of our self-esteem, was attached to our labels and to the validation that they bring. When these labels no longer apply, or when their meaning is significantly altered, our perception of who we are may be fundamentally altered. Who do we become?

Through my trials I have created a new label for myself: writer. On that cold, rainy night in a hotel room in Tamworth when I first launched my thoughts into the world, I could not have conceived just how much of a blessing writing was to become for me. It has helped me to make sense of who I am during a tumultuous time: making sense of becoming a stranger where once I was a husband; becoming a single dad where once I was just dad, and becoming mentally ill where once I was well. Becoming a different me to who I used to be.

The act of writing has been hugely cathartic and once the act of writing is done what remains on the page becomes independent of me, to the extent that it can seem as though it was written by somebody else. When reading it back, it offers an objectivity that wasn't always there previously.

When I'm writing I don't have to worry about the connection being lost between my brain and my fingers in the way that I experience a shutdown in communications between my brain and my mouth. When I'm writing, my unconscious takes over and my words spring forth on the page; it is more likely to result in a, 'Wow! Did I really write that?' than the, 'Wow, did I really say that?' that can accompany what comes out of my mouth at times. Writing is my purest form of expression. When I write it feels like 'this is who I am, this is my voice'.

It is a wonderful thing to find something in your life that offers you moments where everything feels right in the world, where nothing else seems to matter other than what you are doing right here, right now. Something that gives you a buzz, a natural high. For me, nothing quite compares to the feeling of completing a piece of writing, of seeing my thoughts clearly articulated on the screen. The act of creating something from nothing, a creation that depends on nothing and nobody but me.

Why do I share my life in this way? Why be so presumptuous as to think that anybody else will care about my life, my dramas, what I have to say? Well, it isn't really about me, is it? It is not so much my life that I am sharing but the universal experiences of love, loss, pain, hope and a search for meaning, those things that make us so brilliantly, so beautifully, so bewilderingly human. By looking through the lens of my life and writing about these universals, I have found connection with wonderful new people that I would not have known otherwise. I have found meaning amidst hurt and confusion. I have been given opportunities that are helping me to turn the bad in my life into good.

I hope that in some small way, by sharing my writing I can help others to do the same.

EPILOGUE

'LOVE IS A TEMPORARY MADNESS'

On my wedding day I gave a reading, from the wonderful novel 'Captain Corelli's Mandolin' by Louis de Bernieres. The passage asserts that love is a temporary madness that erupts and subsides. The author distinguishes between being 'in love' and love itself, which is what is left after 'being in love' has burned away. At this point we must make a decision as to whether our roots are so entwined that it is unthinkable that we should be apart. For when the blossoms have fallen, those whose roots grow towards each other shall be not two trees but one.

My faith in the truth of this passage, and my trust that I will one day experience such a love in my own life, remains.

WHEN THE LOVE STOPS: PART 2

I stand here now
Got through somehow
A brand new life I'm making
The past recedes
Just memories
The future, mine for taking

ABOUT THE AUTHOR

Matthew Williams is an author and blogger. He lives in the North East of England with his two young children. He is passionate about positive change and turning life's challenges into lessons for creating a better future. He hopes that by writing about his own experiences he will be able to inspire others to make positive changes in their lives.

Something Changed is his first book.

More of Matthew's writing can be found at his blog,
Love, Laughter & Truth, at
www.lovelaughtertruthblog.com

You can follow Matthew on Twitter @3DMathW